MICHAEL

A COPY FOR YOU – ENJOY!

RM
1/8/09

ISBN 978 061 526 7548

Vermont C.O.

The Truth of Attrition

Ryan Mason

This book is dedicated to all the state employees who have endured harassment from their employer.

“All that is necessary for the triumph of evil is for good men to do nothing.”

Edmund Burk

Acknowledgements

The following is a partial list of individuals and organizations that helped make this document possible. Their multiple contributions and guidance have assisted in the completion of this project. I extend my sincerest gratitude to the following:

Robert Bohn for his editorial counsel

The American Correctional Association, (*ACA*) for its continuing contribution in researching data specific to the topic of this book.

The National Institute of Corrections (*NIC*) for also assisting in research specific to this document's completion.

The numerous participants of the NIC Community Corrections Roundtable for their time and input with comparative data.

The Vermont Department of Human Resources for data pertinent to the attrition rates of correctional officers in Vermont

Forward

In May of 2005 the State of Vermont completed its first official report on "*Factors Contributing to the High Attrition Rates of Correctional Officers.*" This report addressed the state's legacy of remarkably high attrition rates for its' first year correctional officers. When examining the attrition rates for the past ten years, a *prima facie* glance may lead one to believe that the attrition rates have decreased. While this may seem to be an improvement, a more scrupulous eye will reveal otherwise.

With further research, it was discovered that the attrition rate for first year correctional officers in the State of Vermont has a permanent seat at the top of the list of "*Turnover rates for classified job titles*" as published by the Vermont Department of Human Resources. In fact, according to the Vermont Department of Human Resources, the number of correctional officers that leave their position in their first year in Vermont consistently exceeds any other position. The percentages are misleading to say the least. For example, in 2006 the attrition rate was an even 30.0%. The actual number of correctional officers loosing their position at 30.0% was 374 while in 2007 the percentage dropped to 23.8 % lowering the number by only five officers, bringing the total to 369 officers lost for that year. This was one of the few years the rate actually dropped. The percentages have mislead us to believe the overall attrition rate as dropping when in fact the actual number of officers leaving their positions within their first year has steadily increased.

According to the American Correctional Association's *2006 Adult and Juvenile Correctional Departments, Institutions, Agencies, and Probation and Parole Authorities Directory*, the State of Vermont reported a turnover rate of only 15.1%

in 2006. Upon a closer look, however, the asterisk indicated that the figure encompassed "all correctional staff" and not just officers. This in itself dramatically lowers the figure as office and support staffs do not have as high a turnover rate as correctional officers. The 2005 ACA Directory did not publish Vermont's attrition rate for that year because, according to the ACA, the state did not provide the information. When research staff scrutinized published attrition data for correctional officers in Vermont for 2005 however, they noticed the Vermont Department of Human Resources published the rate as being 38.4% which did not correspond to the state's own 2005 report which claimed temporary officers turning over at 77% within their first year and 35% for permanent officers. Why such discrepancies?

The National Institute of Corrections (*NIC*) posts an on-line forum called the *Community Corrections Roundtable*. The author received numerous responses to a request for any information regarding attrition rates of correctional officers. Participants nationwide of the Community Corrections Roundtable overwhelmingly suggested that the attrition rates for correctional officers in their respective states were exceedingly high AND often times were attributed to factors outside of their interaction with the inmates. One participant stated that "Officers are promoted into management by the "buddy-buddy" system." Another mentioned that "Most correctional officers do not have a college education and don't care for officers that are trying to go to school."

When compared to any other state employment, for well over the past twelve years, the attrition rate for first year correctional officers in the State of Vermont has not only far exceeded any other turnover rate in the state, but has steadily increased.

Preface

I was about two months into the process of getting my high school teaching license when a neighbor mentioned to me that the Vermont Department of Corrections was hiring correctional officers. He mentioned that because I have a degree in criminal justice, it would be a good fit, and maybe I could use it as a "stepping stone" to further my teaching career. While I had no real deep seeded aspirations to become a correctional officer, I needed the work and the money and benefits were good so I thought, why not apply.

Sure enough, my on-line application was accepted and I was invited to the initial group interview and "New Hire Testing." The initial group interview is the second part of a three part process involving candidates for new correctional officers. After watching a video and completing a written test, each candidate introduced themselves to the group and presented their reasons for wanting to become a correctional officer. After our presentations, several veteran correctional staff presented their own dialogues to the group on what it was like being a correctional officer.

It was here that the Chief of Security from Chittenden Regional Correctional Facility spoke to us about the challenges of working within the "correctional environment." The Chief of Security is the highest ranking uniformed officer in the facility. He mentioned that the job of being a correctional officer was very difficult and that he has seen many rookie officers "not make it" because of the challenges involved in dealing with inmates. The Chief accentuated this point as to make sure we understood the tasks entailed were very difficult.

The Chief of Security then went on to say "Out of the last class graduated from the Academy, eight out of ten working here did not make it past their first year." This immediately struck a chord with me because the rate of eight out of ten officers not making it past their first year seemed excessive. I thought, "Maybe the number was a little exaggerated?" Since he encouraged us to ask questions I raised my hand. Surprised, I asked "Eight out of ten?" The Chief responded by affirming, "Yes, eight out of ten." Applicants both in front and in back of me looked around in amazement. We were all thinking the same thing. How can the Vermont Correctional Academy produce officers where eight out of ten don't make it past their first year? When another applicant asked the Chief, "What contributed to the demise of those eight officers," he responded, "They were all caught or implicated with bringing in contraband."

This was alarming. Several other applicants also expressed their concern. While we didn't want to question the validity of the veteran Chief, something just seemed a little "off." How could eight out of ten correctional officers be so naïve or persuaded to smuggle contraband, whether it be drugs or tobacco into a correctional facility? I thought to myself, maybe three out of ten or even four. But how could 80% of a newly graduated class of correctional officers hired at one particular correctional facility be persuaded to commit a felony for criminals? How could that many officers fall afoul of their duties so severely? I was soon to have an answer.

Table of Contents

The following is documentation of how the State of Vermont covers up corruption and promotes the industrialization of its own Correctional Academy which is the institution responsible for training correctional officers in the State of Vermont.

The events described herein are the experiences of a correctional officer who worked for the Vermont State Department of Corrections in Burlington, Vermont from December 2006 until August 2007. The author and former correctional officer holds a degree in criminal justice and was hoping to pursue his Master's in the same field. He is a former assistant professor at the University Law School Jean Moulin, Lyon 3 in Lyon France (92-96,) where he taught the U.S. Constitution to second-year law students. The author also completed his post graduate dissertations, at the International Organization of Criminal Police, Interpol world headquarters with emphasis on "cultural assimilations" in the field of criminal justice.

This document was created with much trepidation as the home of the author and former correctional officer is less than one mile from the facility in which he worked. Since his separation from the Vermont D.O.C. he has had numerous experiences with individuals he's identified at the facility, both inmates and staff. During this same time period, his family's property and vehicles have been vandalized numerous times. Correctional officers have followed him to his place of employment and approached him under the pretext of good will. It appears they did this specifically for the purposes of locating his employment as to continue their attack on him. His family has lived at the same residence for over thirty years and until now, never once had to worry about their security. Most of these events have been occurring posterior to his separation from the Vermont D.O.C. One of them however, occurred during his employment, so he mentioned the incident to his then-supervisor (a 29-year veteran of the facility) who chuckled and said, "Just deal with it as you would anything else."

It is not the intent of the writer to place blame on any one or group of individual(s), but rather to expose a corrupt system which has been left unchecked by the State of Vermont. Here the writer will describe how he was singled out at the Vermont Correctional Academy and once graduated, deliberately and repeatedly set up to fail by his fellow officers at the facility where he was employed. From his graduation at the VCA (*Vermont Correctional Academy*) on February 2nd, 2007, until he separated from the Department of Corrections in August of 2007 he accounts for over nineteen separate incidences of harassment by his own peers at his place of employment.

In what appears to be an ongoing effort to justify or explain their own misconduct, well posterior to his employment at the Vermont DOC, state officials have waged an active smear campaign against the former CO within his own community. The results of this campaign are so reprehensible that they include openly paying him less than others for the same job performed, and for what he was hired for, at the school where he is part time employed. This State sponsored "Black Listing" has thrown up so many extra obstacles for him to overcome that it's now virtually next to impossible for him to return to his original profession of teaching for which he is highly qualified. This demonstrates how the State can still successfully attack the former CO well after his employment has ended.

The "Whistle Blower"

In its entirety, article sixty-seven of the *Vermont State Employees' Association Handbook for the Corrections Bargaining Unit*, states the following:

> "**1**. A WHISTLE BLOWER is defined as a person covered by this agreement who makes public allegations of inefficiency or impropriety in government. No provision of this agreement shall be deemed to interfere with such an employee in the exercise of his or her constitutional rights of free speech, and such persons shall not be discriminated against in this employment with regard thereto."
>
> "**2**. The protections provided by this Article do not apply to an employee whose statements are made with malicious disregard of the truth."
>
> "**3**. Employees who possess information about inefficiency or impropriety in state government are urged to bring that information to the attention of appropriate officials prior to making public allegations."

In retrospect, the former Correctional Officer, or "CO" as they are referred to, believes that he was profiled as a potential "whistle blower" and therefore targeted by numerous veteran staff at the facility in which he worked to deliberately impede his job performance so that he would be dismissed prior to him exposing any illicit activity at the facility. The illicit activity he refers to is being committed and covered up by the correctional staff itself. It is not determined whether or not this activity is being conducted in conjunction with, or separate from, the inmate population. It is possible that veteran correctional staff have learned how to manipulate the environment in which they work to profit from their activities.

The former CO sincerely supports the overall "stated mission" of the Vermont Correctional Academy. He does not intend to aimlessly criticize the Vermont Department of Corrections nor undermine the enormous task of housing and caring for criminals. Much time and effort was spent on compiling this documentation as to ensure the most accurate portrayal of events be brought forth with the intent of exposing the flagrant abuse of Vermont's most valuable resource, its employees.

As in numerous other states, the State of Vermont has a "six-month probationary period" for most of its state employees. This period is designed to be a working test period as to ensure their employment is a proper "fit" and to safeguard against any "problem employees" or, in this case, someone who would expose a potential racket or wrongdoing at the state level. During this initial six-month period, the incumbent CO may be terminated for any reason or no reason at all.

Even if the new CO elects from the beginning of employment to be a paying member of the Vermont State Employees Association, during their first six months, they will have absolutely no recourse whatsoever, even if they are repeatedly harassed by the very staff that is supposedly there to support and train them. Veteran correctional staff learned how to manipulate the probationary period to not only discriminate against and harass new employees but most likely cover up illicit activity, either that committed by inmates or by correctional staff itself. It is here that the new or Rookie CO will be profiled by his peers as someone who will either go along with the activity or "Blow the Whistle," as described in the state employee handbook.

After the Rookie realized that he was being harassed, he was able to contact his state employee representative who confirmed that, as he was still in his "Initial six-month probationary period, there was nothing that he could do to curb the harassment." "So what does one do if they're being harassed during this time period," the Rookie asked? Again she said, "There's very little you can do." So after conferring with family and friends in view of all of these circumstances in their entirety, he has decided to document his experience with the hope of bringing the issues of harassment and corruption in Vermont state government to the public's attention and to the attention of any prospective employees.

The not so humble pretext that many correctional officers will give us is that "It's a tough job, and it's not for everyone." What they don't want you and I to know is, that its potentially fellow correctional staff making it tough for new employees, not the inmates, as they'd rather have you believe.

The former correctional officer worked between 44-72 hours a week in whatever units he was assigned. He never requested an easy assignment and did whatever his superiors asked with more than due diligence. He was eager to prove his work ethic and never once questioned his supervisors unless he was being trained in a new task and needed clarification. His attitude was positive and cooperative all the time. Even after it became apparent to him that he was being deliberately set up to fail by his fellow staff, he did not let it affect his positive attitude or desire to work. In fact, this motivated him to work even harder, and he started requesting overtime to cover for those who called in absent. Since the Rookie CO lived near the facility, it was easier for him to work overtime than it was for his peers who lived further away. He has since learned that other staff accused him of "hawking" the overtime. "Hawking" is a term used to describe someone who has diligently sought to acquire a specific goal, the way a hawk would hover over and stalk its prey. The term is employed by those who have become opposed to the person(s) achieving their goal. Yet the supervisors calling him to see if he could come in to cover the empty staffing, always seemed pleased to have him as a standby to cover for them.

Many veteran CO's develop long-term relationships with inmates who are either serving long sentences, or who are repeat offenders referred to as *recidivists*, enabling the staff to use their influence over certain inmates to make the job of the new CO more difficult.

This is a two-way street, in fact. If veteran correctional staff found a rookie correctional officer to be desirable for whatever reason, they would deliberately set the rookie up to succeed in numerous ways, just as they would to set a rookie up to fail. The manipulation of inmate populations by their custodial correctional staff for their own profit is nothing new. This has been going on for centuries, and unfortunately for the State of Vermont, it continues today.

This collusion is what the writer refers to as a "Cultural Assimilation" between the minority correctional staff and the majority inmate population in their custody. Let us be clear that it is the correctional staff assimilating to the inmate population and not the other way around. If one rubs elbows long enough with someone else, no matter who they are, at some point that person would begin to reflect the other person's behaviors in some way or another, whether they like it or not. Another similar type of assimilation is the "Stockholm Syndrome," in which a hostage or captive shows signs of loyalty to the hostage-taker as demonstrated by heiress Patty Hearst during her kidnapping in the 1970's.

The 2005 *Report on Factors Contributing to High Attrition Rates of Correctional Officers,* corroborated this on page twenty-six highlighting a CO narrative stating; "They tell us that we teach the offender pro-social skills. With a 50 to 1 ratio, who's learning what from whom? Correctional Staff are just as 'institutionalized' as offenders who max out a sentence."

Within the correctional environment, the custodial correctional staff is the minority and yet must maintain the cooperation of and complete control over their inmate population, the majority. To gain the cooperation of the inmates, correctional staff has a variety of methods and avenues from which to choose. Just a few examples are the deterrence of being sent to the segregation unit which in this case is Alpha unit. Most inmates who behave have the opportunity to move into privileged units where they are allowed to have jobs, visits, more commissary items, and additional inside and outside recreation.

The writer and former correctional officer does not pretend to be an authority on all the issues affecting the Department of Corrections in Vermont. He does however, lay claim as a first-hand witness to the corruption and community character assassination of its former employees as well as the deliberate industrialization of correctional officers that exist in the State of Vermont. Let's face it, if the attrition rate of correctional officers goes down, what's going to happen to the number of newly hired CO's at the Vermont Correctional Academy?

This is what will happen. The need for the Vermont Correctional Academy's CO classes will decrease as the need for newly trained correctional officers goes down.

The only other known report on this subject in Vermont was completed in May of 2005 by a team of four state employees called the V.P.M. or the *Vermont Performance Manager's Consulting Team* who were not employed by the Department of Corrections but by other various state agencies. Their work, "*Factors Contributing to the High Attrition Rates of Correctional Officers,*" found that a turnover rate of 35% for first-year correctional officers existed for permanent employees and a rate of 77% existed for temporary correctional officers. This makes for an overall attrition rate of 56% for newly hired CO's. This report was based primarily on staff employment surveys which were compiled into a results oriented document allowing suggestions for improvement. This report found that the monetary cost for that year, in training alone, for CO's who left in less than one year totaled approximately $500,000.

The Vermont Correctional Academy or VCA

The former correctional officer remembers vividly while at the Academy the then-president of the Academy announcing to his class of new recruits that "CO's are dropping like flies!" What they don't want the public to know is why, "they're dropping like flies." The inmates, unfortunately, don't have as much to do with it as one would think, and if they do play a role, chances are they may have been influenced or motivated by the correctional staff *mis en gard* [put in place] to watch over them.

The former correctional officer recalls that from the beginning of his classes at the VCA, he and one other recruit were singled out in front of the entire class as being the only two college graduates with four-year college degrees. How could this be a bad thing? Well much to his surprise, the former CO's college degree may have been a key contributor in making him a desirable target amongst the staff who were there to support and train him. Despite all his own efforts to cast aside any notion of mal intent on behalf of the Vermont Correctional Academy, he'll describe the events to the very best of his own ability and as objectively as possible to allow the reader to decide for themselves.

During the first day of his classes at the Academy, located at the College of St. Joseph just outside Rutland, Vermont his class was being introduced to the three administrators of the Academy: Mark Perkins, Peter Spence and Dr. Rodrigez. After the general opening formalities of the Academy were complete and each of the administrators addressed the responsibilities of the recruits, as normal, they divided the class into three squads: Alpha, Bravo and Charlie. Each squad had a squad leader, creating a semi-or para-military cohesion for them to work in. After that the Rookie CO remembered Dr. Rodrigez was at the podium discussing statistics concerning correctional officers in the State of Vermont. As the new recruit held a BS degree in criminal justice he listened in admiration to what Dr. Rodrigez had to say. Dr. Rodrigez earned his Ph.D. in criminal justice, and the Rookie remembered thinking of him as a positive example and role model for him to follow since he might someday pursue his Ph.D. in the same field.

At the end of his talk, Dr. Rodrigez then asked the class if there are "any individuals here with a four-year college degree?" The only other person with a four-year degree was also in the Rookie's squad, and they both raised their hands. Thinking that they might have some extra responsibility or be asked to meet with one of the administrators later on, they thought nothing of it. But then, this is exactly what happened. Without any exaggeration, when the Rookie CO and the only other person with a degree in the class raised their hands, they both noticed Dr. Rodrigez glanced over at Mark Perkins, who then looked at Peter Spence, who in turn gave a serious look back at him. It was a bizarre moment in that all three made note of who had raised their hands and then said nothing.

At that point the two Rookie CO's immediately and simultaneously lowered their hands. Trust in the writer, as one almost had to be there to feel that something was out of place. It was as if the question were asked to see if there'd be any problems or issues, instead of as an assessment of the recruits' credentials. After that segment of the class and during the break that followed, the former CO conferred with his squad mate and only other degree holder about the question that Dr. Rodrigez had asked them in front of the class. He agreed that the response of the administrators to them raising their hands in acknowledgement of their prior education was totally unexpected, and if they had to answer the question again under those circumstances, both agreed they would have **denied** their credentials, even if it meant lying about their education. But the Rookie CO knew they already had a copy of his resume articulating his education in detail. How many people would ever lie about having gone to college, and particularly, about graduating? In this case, the CO's BS in criminal justice was a good match for a correctional officer, right? Well, that's what one would think.

Unfortunately and whether or not intentionally, the administrators not only singled out the only two college-educated individuals in that class of the VCA, but, as the writer will describe later, targeted them in numerous ways.

It's been said that it costs the State of Vermont about $7,000. per recruit to send each to the Vermont Correctional Academy. When the Rookie attended, the Academy lasted six weeks. Each week, a different visiting correctional officer or health instructor would teach various subjects from *Use of Force, CPR* to *Advanced Communication Techniques* (*ACT*), to name a few. This was actually nice because it allowed the recruits to familiarize themselves with different veterans in the field. Since the Department of Corrections in Vermont is under the Agency of Human Services, there were a variety of other instructors, not just correctional staff. At the end of six weeks, each recruit was expected to pass all subjects after a total of 200 hours of VCA instruction required by the State.

During many of the role-play animations practicing the communication techniques for CO's to use on inmates, the instructor would play, or act out as the inmate, and it would be the responsibility of the recruit to stand up in front of the class and use the techniques he had learned, practicing employing them on the instructors posing as inmates. WELL who do you think got the most difficult and abusive inmate scenarios out of the entire class? Not once, not twice, not three or four times, but repeatedly did several of the instructors bare down much more on the college grads than on anyone else in the class. They didn't want to complain as they thought it might be a test of some kind. Their observations were confirmed when several of the other recruits approached them at different and separate times to say that they, too, noticed that the instructors used their most violent and verbally abusive inmate profiles on just them. When it was time for the college graduates to demonstrate their application of the learned communication techniques, the instructors playing the inmates made it notably more difficult for them in that they applied much more resistance, yelling profanities and insults at the recruits the same way a mentally distraught inmate would, making a spectacle of them in front of the class. Several of their classmates said in their own words, "Boy, they really had it out for you!" Many of the women and other recruits were left with some of the easiest scenarios out of the whole week of classes. The two college grads weren't in a position to complain or even mention their observations, as it would have been a pretext to process them out of the Academy. They were already starting to feel targeted. They knew that this was part of the job: they just didn't think it would be coming from the staff that was purportedly there to support and train them. It was almost as if to say "So you think you're so special, college boy? We'll see about that." They were literally going after them. The two Rookie CO's never once gave the VCA staff any reason to target them. They never bragged nor boasted and kept a low profile. They kept their mouths shut and their heads down.

There was one individual in their squad that had trouble learning the new material, and even though many of his fellow classmates including the writer's additional help, failed out during the fourth week of classes. This was unfortunate, but after a certain point of sacrificing their own time to assist him, they couldn't allow the extra burden to diminish their own grades. The writer mentions this because the instructor from that week was a man with many years of experience, Jerry Rickter. The writer had much respect for Mr. Rickter because he knew his subjects cold and was easy going. Mr. Rickter seemed to be someone who was serious about teaching his recruits and honestly wanted his students to succeed. When Mr. Rickter inquired of the former CO about the poor performance of the classmate who had trouble with the new material, the former CO explained in detail which of the classmates had spent extra time with this individual (including himself) and that it had gotten to the point where the time he spent assisting the recruit was detrimental to his own performance. At that, Mr. Rickter said that he understood and wasn't aware of all their efforts to help the recruit with his studies. He seemed sincere when the former COs explained this. It was unfortunate, however, that Mr. Rickter used this event with the underachiever to do more damage to the Rookie CO than Mr. Rickter probably anticipated.

The FILE

Section 2 Concerning *Employee Personnel Records* of Article 11 of the *Vermont State Employees' Association Handbook for the Corrections Bargaining Unit* states that;

> "With the exception of material that is confidential or privileged under law, an employee will be allowed access to his/her official personnel file during normal working hours. Subject to the exception stated above, copies of all documents and materials placed in an employee's official personnel file after July 1, 1986, are to be given, on a one-time basis, to the employee at no cost to the employee."

At the VCA each recruit has a file that the instructors compile as the coursework progresses. Should the recruit graduate from the Academy, this file goes on to the CO's facility for their supervisors to examine. So whatever is written about the employee is passed on and scrutinized by whomever, to pass judgment on them as they feel fit. If a recruit comes across as too arrogant or as not having enough confidence, they'll write about it in their file. How they write about a recruit may very well determine whether or not they succeed.

In terms of the facility the CO ends up working at, it narrows down to this: if they want a CO to succeed, **they will**, if they don't, **they won't**. The **real** reasons for veteran staff wanting a Rookie CO to succeed or not may never be known fully. In fact, certain veteran staff will go to great lengths to cover up these real reasons. They'll use other well-known pretexts such as, "It's just not for everyone" or "They weren't a good fit."

While working at the correctional facility, the Rookie CO began wondering what might have been written about him. Knowing that he had at least one positive feedback from another CO, the Rookie thought that it would be a good idea to take a look at his file to see what was there. In the Vermont Department of Corrections, an "S1" is the title designation for a supervisor who is above a CO I and COII. S1 Jake Milford told the Rookie that he could view his file whenever he wanted.

On July 30th 2007, when the Rookie went to ask the office manager if the positive feedbacks were included in his supervisor's file, she said that the positive feedbacks were usually kept in a different file from the supervisor's file which kept any reprimand, write up, or negative comment. The Rookie made note of this because this meant that the facility separated the positive and negative feedbacks into separate files. This didn't make any sense. He didn't question her knowledge nor her authority; he just inquired about seeing his file and if it would have all the feedback and observations as it had at the Academy. From what the office manager told him, it would not. The Rookie wanted to see if his file was, to his mind, accurate and if there were any remarks noted in it since his graduation from the Academy. Why would they keep the positive feedbacks separate from the supervisor's file? It seemed strange to him that the state would deliberately separate the positive remarks from the negative remarks into separate files. It would be like having two incomplete files on someone, thus misleading any potential reader. This would not only leave much room for discrepancy but defeat the purpose of having a file in the first place.

The Rookie CO had asked his S1 and the office manager several times if he'd be allowed to see his file. The responses he received were varied and usually resulted in the subject being dropped. The Rookie did not want to push the subject because he knew that he was still in his initial six-month probation and did not want to create a scene nor any tensions with the administration.

Once he was finally allowed to examine his file he was astonished to find that Mr. Rickter had written exactly the opposite about the Rookie's efforts to assist his classmate with his studies. Even though the former CO thoroughly explained his efforts and Mr. Rickter appeared to acknowledge his efforts verbally, he wrote the MOST potentially damaging and slanderous version in his file. Whether or not he acted with malice or not is unclear. But to whomever would read this Rookie CO's file about this affair would most certainly be misled. This not only undermines the moral integrity of the former CO but is yet another example of how the Academy deliberately set this individual up to fail. In fact, much of the file was atrocious. It was easy to see why the facility didn't want him to read his file. It was appalling. One of the instructors wrote "He thinks he better than everyone else." This fallacious statement is yet another example of how the Academy deliberately set him up to fail.

When the recruit asked about his file at the Academy, most of the staff played it off as nothing to worry about. Little did they want him to know apparently. Whoever was to read this file would most certainly have come away with a very tainted and untrue perception of this individual.

"A Game of Inches"

While in his fourth week at the Academy the Rookie CO finally realized that he and the only other college graduate were being targeted excessively. Therefore, the Rookie thought it would be a good idea to meet with the president of the Academy (Mr. Perkins) to ask for advice on how to better improve their standing as new recruits, thus increasing their chances at graduating from the Academy.

The VCA, as many organizations, boasts an "Open Door" policy for individuals who need to reach out to the administration to communicate concerns, should they feel the need to do so. So the Rookie asked Mr. Perkins if it would be okay to meet with him in his office after classes to ask for advice on how he (the Rookie) might improve his candidature at becoming a CO for the Vermont D.O.C.. In order to meet with Mr. Perkins, the Rookie had to pass through another office, leading to the president's office. In this adjacent office, a training CO II officer was at the desk. The door to Mr. Perkins's office was open, and even though Mr. Perkins said he could close the door if the Rookie wanted, the Rookie didn't have anything to hide, so he declined.

The Rookie started by praising the Academy and telling the president that he felt fortunate to be apart of the 88th graduating class of the VCA. The Rookie then said, however, that he felt that maybe he and the other college graduate had perhaps drawn a little too much of the wrong kind of attention and wanted to know if the president could give him some advice on how to better prepare for graduation. The Rookie said that he respected Mr. Perkins's years in corrections and hoped that Mr. Perkins could maybe council him on improving his profile as a Rookie CO.

The President asked the Rookie, "What do you want out of all this? What are your career goals?" Not wanting to be too presumptuous, the Rookie responded by saying that he first wanted to graduate from the VCA. "And then?" responded Mr. Perkins. The Rookie said he wanted to complete his initial six-month probationary period at the facility and see from there. The president said, "And if you do, what then?" The Rookie said that he was hoping to return to his original profession of teaching someday and that he was currently enrolled in Vermont's Alternative Licensure Program for Peer Review. Mr. Perkins said that there were teaching positions available in the D.O.C. and various other state agencies. The Rookie acknowledged his suggestions and also said that there was a local college in Burlington that had a criminal justice program where he was hoping to become an adjunct. The Rookie said that he hoped to expand on his teaching experience when he taught overseas except in this case for American students of criminal justice. The Rookie's first career was teaching second year French law students the U.S. Constitution in Lyon, France. He thought that by becoming a CO he could maybe teach for the state or the local college which was within walking distance from his home. Mr. Perkins said, "That local college is a booming place." The president was referring to the fact that the local college was growing tremendously and had more and more students each year.

Mr. Perkins was polite and said that there were "two things that stood out in his mind" concerning the Rookie CO. The first thing was that he (Mr. Perkins) reminded the Rookie CO that "This is a game of inches." The Rookie acknowledged his remark and allowed the president to explain that one does not want to seem "too hungry" and that the Rookie should concentrate on graduating first. The Rookie thanked him and agreed, stating "That's why I said I wanted to graduate first". Mr. Perkins said, "You get there one step at a time. No big leaps." The Rookie said that he hoped he hadn't come off as a "know it all" because he had much to learn. The second thing the president had to recommend for the Rookie was this: The president said that the Rookie said something that stood out in the president's mind. The word that the Rookie said which was the second part of the president's advice was "Humble." The Rookie smiled and said "Yes, humble." The president of the Academy said, "Those two things are what I'm thinking will help you get through this."

So after a few more pleasantries and small talk, the Rookie reiterated what the president said, as to not forget. The president politely acknowledged the Rookie's affirmation with a smile. The Rookie recruit thanked the president for his time and advice. The Rookie thought to himself: "At least he knows I'm serious about graduating and doesn't think I'm a know it all."

Five months after this event, when the Rookie was allowed to see his file, he read a full page of libelous remarks about his meeting, not from the president but from the officer in the adjacent office who apparently took full advantage of his trust and openness to eavesdrop on their meeting. To the Rookie CO's complete horror, it was if the officer listening in on their meeting was somehow jealous or had a "bone to pick" with the recruit for him to write such defamations of his character. Unfortunately, the Rookie wasn't allowed to make a copy of this file for his own record. He could see why the Vermont Department of Corrections might not want him to have a copy. In the Rookie's mind the remarks were nothing short of character defamation.

The Rookie remembered seeing a photocopy of one of his timecards with the two times he was late highlighted. He remembered seeing Mr. Richter's page describing the antithesis of what actually happened with the Rookie helping his classmate with his academics. The File contained only bad things about the Rookie and to the best of the Rookie's recollection it did not contain one good thing at all about him.

For him to document his listening in on someone else's meeting and then include it in this individual's file demonstrates a certain vigor with little regard for the eavesdropping officer's own integrity particularly since there was not one bad thing at all about the meeting. The meeting was completely positive and allowed Mr. Perkins to give the Rookie CO the sound advice that he sought. This demonstrates willingness by certain correctional staff to misrepresent truthful events by misleading the readers of the supervisors "File." Here it was done with deliberate character defamation or what the former Rookie CO deems a completely different perception of what actually transpired in the meeting.

The Rookie's only hypotheses about this type of activity on behalf of the state of Vermont are that maybe it is a way to "thin the ranks" of aspiring CO's or to locate "potentially problem employees" prior to them graduating from the Academy. To the best of the Rookie's recollection, none of his instructors nor VCA administrators ever used this file to help him improve his CO skills or chances of graduating from the Academy. The sad reality was that the file was being compiled to build a case to dismiss him instead of help him.

The truth is that during the Rookie CO's first five months he behaved with such humility that the number one criticism of his performance by his supervisors was that "he needs more self confidence."

Oleoresin Capsicum (OC)

Oleoresin Capsicum or "OC" is the technical name for what many refer to as "Mace" or "pepper spray." This item is legally considered a "non-lethal or less than lethal weapon" because it won't kill or dismember the target individual(s), (or shouldn't anyway). The use of "OC" is designed to immobilize its targets or victims so that the officers involved may prevent them from escape, self harm or harming someone else, thus allowing them to be apprehended or taken into custody. OC was developed by Gardner L. Whitcomb in 1976 and has been produced in various strengths by several different companies.

The word "Oleoresin" refers to a mixture of an essential oil or resin which is found in nature. In other words, it's an oil-based product and cannot be washed off easily. The word "Capsicum" refers to the oil of Capsicum or common hot pepper of the garden. Yes, it's all natural. Usually this ingredient is some concentration of the cayenne pepper. While using OC, recruits learn to target the face and more specifically, the mouth and eyes of a target. Being sprayed with OC is immobilizing because its effects involve extreme burning sensations and inflammation of the eyes, mucous membranes, and contaminated skin, thus rendering its victims temporarily incapacitated, blinded and painfully uncomfortable.

One of the weeks (or segments) of classes at the VCA was spent on "Use of Force." Correctional officers are in daily contact with violent or potentially violent individuals who may pose a threat to themselves or those around them. Pepper spray, Mace, or "OC" whether aerosol, streamer, or foam is one tool correctional officers have at their disposal to inhibit or neutralize such threats. During the "Use of Force" segment, CO recruits learn a variety of defensive tactics, handcuffing procedures, take down and cell extraction protocols. The end of this segment entailed being sprayed with "OC." For some recruits, this was probably the only real stressful part of the VCA because they openly didn't want to be sprayed with the oil-based contaminant.

The Rookie CO had been trained previously with "OC" or pepper spray during his lethal and non-lethal weapons certification in the state of Pennsylvania where he received his BS in criminal justice. He was also trained in "OC" at the Burlington Police Department, in Burlington, Vermont when he completed his undergraduate internship with the city Police department. The Rookie remembered that his training was completed very professionally. The trainers in Pennsylvania were instructors from the Pennsylvania State Police and knew how to motivate their students. They put the students at ease by conveying to them that they took no pleasure in the actual application of the "OC" to their trainees. It was as if the instructors themselves loathed the application as well, instead of enjoying it. The trainer he had at the Burlington Police Department during his undergraduate internship was a veteran of the police force from the time dating well prior to the invention of "OC." Despite what we now might consider being "Old School," these trainers were truly professional and were not training individuals for any other reason other than it was part of their job, and wanted to help train individuals on the use of "OC."

The trainers the Rookie had at the VCA were supposedly professional, too; this however, is what happened. As the "OC" class came to an end, as expected, the VCA recruits prepared themselves to experience being sprayed with "OC." Each recruit was given a "OC training consent form" which included a brief medical questionnaire and waiver agreement for the recruit to sign prior to being sprayed. During the days leading up to the spraying of the recruits, the Rookie overheard several conversations between various recruits and the instructors about how the recruits were to be sprayed. The VCA instructors calmly put the inquisitors' minds at easy by saying that "they just do a quick squirt across your forehead."

The Rookie remembered hearing the two use-of-force instructors say openly to the youngest of the class that he was going to "get it first." The youngest of the Rookie's class had served as a CO in another state. This recruit may have drawn more attention to himself because many of his questions during the Academy involved his prior experiences as a correctional officer. He was also a light-hearted and cheerful individual who may have rubbed the "Use of Force" trainers the wrong way as the "class clown."

During one of the cell extraction exercises that week the Rookie stood by the instructors as they watched the youngest of their class during his execution of the extraction. The Rookie noticed the discontentment on the faces of the instructors. The Rookie wasn't the only recruit standing nearby as others would watch the extraction exercises while they progressed. The Rookie noticed that when the youngest of his class was just a little over zealous with one of his restraining maneuvers the instructors both said, "He shouldn't be here." In this case "He" meant the youngest of their class. They targeted him.

The Rookie remembered how he was trained before and he remembered that he was not directly sprayed in the eyes nor face, but the instructors had the recruits line up and would "dab" their cheeks with liberal amounts of OC and ordered each to "go" so the next recruit could get his dose. This method of applying the OC was more than what was needed as OC is oil-based and a good two-finger dab on the cheek would give the recruit the full effect of what it was like to be contaminated with OC.

To the best of the Rookie's knowledge, there were two primary reasons for which law enforcement and correctional officers are sprayed with OC. The first reason was so that in the event the officer needed to use OC in the line of duty and became contaminated himself (which happens often), the officer wouldn't panic and would recognize its affects as mere contamination. The second reason for being sprayed was so that the recruits would then have confidence in the weapon they were wielding. Being sprayed with OC would allow the recruit to feel the immobilizing affects of OC and therefore respect its power.

The Rookie remembered one recruit who came from the north of the state say: "When we have Fire Arms training they don't shoot us, so we know what it feels like to get shot, do they?" The Rookie understood his point, and the instructors were starting to have a little too much fun with the activity of "spraying down the recruits."

The instructors set up a water hose decontaminating station behind one of the dorms at the college. In short, the applications of OC were far from equal. The youngest of the Rookie's class whom the instructors openly targeted got the first dose. Not only was his dose larger than most of the other recruits, but the instructors deliberately used a product called "Red Saber," a red foam type of OC which has the highest amount of Capsicum on the market, of 18%. The instructors sprayed him directly into the eyes, not on the forehead. Starting with his left eye first, then to his right eye, then repeated in a horizontal back and forth motion. The Rookie noticed that many of the women recruits and "class favorites or pets" received lesser doses, on their foreheads with a less potent form of OC. The Rookie wondered if the Vermont Criminal Justice Training Council would approve of this. The instructors said that the instructors themselves needed to be sprayed each time they had their instructor certification renewed. The fact that the instructors had to be sprayed themselves did not really control or restrain their unequal application of OC amongst the recruits.

Further more, that morning prior to going outside to being sprayed, the instructors singled out any recruit that openly did not want to be sprayed by loudly asking the class "Is there anyone here who's not going to be sprayed?" The class knew that if someone did not want to get sprayed, then they did not have to get sprayed. Many recruits asked if their graduation was contingent on being sprayed. However when the instructors asked the class on the day they were getting sprayed if anyone was going to opt out, it was as if to intimidate those who did not want to be sprayed by making a spectacle of them in front of the class. No one dared raise their hand when they asked the class this, but the Rookie could tell there were several there who had issues with it. The Rookie just remained silent and filed through to get his dose. He noticed that Officer Knopp, the CO that interviewed him just happened to show up to witness the recruits being sprayed. The Rookie thought it interesting that the officer who interviewed him, drove two hours to the Academy to witness the OC application to the CO recruits. He was there just for the spraying portion of the exercise. The Rookie wasn't the only recruit that noticed the satisfaction officer Knopp seemed to have from watching the recruits being sprayed.

The Rookie couldn't place his tongue on the word to describe this type of behavior. Then it dawned on him. There was no word in the English language that really described officer Knopp's enjoyment of watching the recruits being sprayed with OC. He learned later that the German vocabulary had a word that is sometimes used in the upper echelons of academic English to describe this type of behavior. The word is *Schadenfreude*. *Schadenfreude* refers to a malicious satisfaction obtained from the misfortune of others. That is what the Rookie was witnessing here when he noticed officer Knopp's appearance for the spraying of the new recruits. The Rookie realized that though it was purely speculative, maybe that was why officer Knopp was a correctional officer. Maybe there was some inner satisfaction he obtained from witnessing the misfortune of others.

With the exception of the only other college graduate dropping out on the second to last day before graduation and the other recruit who failed out academically, the remaining recruits graduated from the VCA on February 2nd 2007, the Rookie with a 91.47 % GPA.

14 College Credits

One of the achievements of the Vermont Correctional Academy was that the Academy had recently been accredited for fourteen college credits through a small upstate New York College in their Criminal Justice Program. What that meant was individuals graduating from the VCA would be entitled to fourteen undergraduate credits in the field of Criminal Justice should they be interested in pursuing their undergraduate degree.

Even though the Rookie already had his Bachelor of Science degree in Criminal Justice, he wondered if it would help him in any way to upgrade his portfolio or transcripts with more recent credits. After the Rookie graduated from the VCA, he inquired of the VCA administration about how to get these college credits. He found out that all he needed to do was pay a fifty-dollar matriculation fee with the small college and those fourteen college credits would be awarded to the VCA graduate. The Rookie realized that this was a good deal for someone who had never graduated with their undergraduate degree. He thought: "Fourteen college credits could cost a lot more than $50." And if you graduated from the VCA within the past five years, you were entitled to these credits. Furthermore, the Rookie realized that numerous other CO's at his facility had attended either community colleges or on-line universities in the hopes of getting their undergraduate degree in criminal justice. Many of the CO's weren't even aware that these fourteen college credits were available to them, and for some CO's, that was all they needed to have finished their four-year degree.

The Rookie CO called the president of the VCA (Mr. Perkins) to ask him about the procedure involved for VCA graduates to receive their fourteen college credits. Mr. Perkins told the Rookie he must contact the college and provide them with a letter from the VCA stating that the CO was indeed a graduate from the VCA. Mr. Hassle said that once the Rookie had all the paperwork in order for the college, to contact the VCA and they would send him the letter. The Rookie asked the president of the VCA why other CO's were not taking advantage of the VCA's accreditation for the fourteen college credits. The Rookie mentioned that in return for the $50.matriculation fee, a CO would be awarded about $6,000.worth of undergraduate credits. As stated earlier, this was all that a CO might need to receive his or her four-year college degree. The president of the VCA responded by saying, "I don't know why more people don't take advantage of it." The president also went on to say, "You'll be the first ever to have initiated this process, and to date, not one graduate of the Academy has ever taken advantage of this accreditation with the college."

At this the Rookie contacted the small upstate New York College for the paperwork needed to pay the fee and verify graduation from the VCA. The Rookie then asked whichever CO's at his facility would be interested in receiving their college credits. Several CO's were very interested in getting the paperwork, so the Rookie made copies and left them in their mailboxes. The Rookie felt good knowing that he was spreading the opportunity for fellow CO's to become graduates of criminal justice as he was a graduate in the same field.

Unfortunately, not all the veteran CO's at his facility shared in his enthusiasm for promoting higher education. The Rookie CO noticed the distain that many veteran CO's had for him while helping his fellow staff receive their credits. On two separate occasions while distributing the paperwork to the mailboxes of the few CO's that expressed interest,

DOC staff balked at that fact he was helping his fellow COs with furthering their education. Maybe this was why no one else had tried to receive the 14 college credits due them from graduating.

Chittenden Regional Correctional Facility

After graduating from the VCA, the Rookie CO was hired as a "permanent, full-time state employee" at the Chittenden Regional Correctional Facility (CRCF) located at 7 Ferral Street in South Burlington, Vermont.

On page twenty-seven of the *2005 Report on Factors Contributing to High Attrition Rates of Correctional Officers* it states with regard to CRCF; "At this facility, there was a strong sentiment that recognition of achievements needed to be more formal and frequent." On the same page the report went on to say; "Several comments indicated that inmates are not held accountable for their actions and that in some cases, inmates were treated better than staff."

On February 5th, the former correctional officer reported for duty, and after a two-week shadow / training period, was assigned to be in Delta Unit for 2nd shift, from 1530-2330 hours or 3:30pm to 11:30pm. Here the Rookie became acclimated to the correctional environment and was able to successfully employ many of the techniques taught to him at the Academy.

As in most correctional facilities, CRCF has its populations divided up into different living units. This is done to better control the inmate populations and to keep security risks to a minimum, since many inmates may not be intermingled or allowed into the facility's general population. For example, sex offenders are often targeted by numerous other types of offenders and for their own security are kept separated into their own living unit.

The Delta Unit had two cameras at that time which were located in the unit day room and at the end of the hallway which had all the doors to the inmates' cells. (The dayroom in a correctional facility's living unit is the single common gathering area within the unit where the inmates may gather, meet, play games or watch television if permitted.) These cameras were fed to the control room, or "bubble" as the inmates called it. For the first five weeks, the new CO ran his unit during second shift with what appeared to be no problem.

THEN during the month of March the first of many incidents occurred that made the writer realize he was being harassed by his fellow correctional officers. At first, the Rookie CO hoped that these first incidents were just his senior CO's joking with him. He thought that maybe it was just a routine type of hazing that rookie CO's tolerated to become a part of the team. That was his hope anyway. In the beginning he didn't really think it was an attempt to deliberately impede his job performance. As he would find out within the next few months, he was wrong.

The DELTA Logbook Incident

The Delta Unit office has two entrances to it. One entryway is from the Delta Unit hallway which is the primary entryway into the office; the other entrance is from the adjacent Echo Unit. There are two windows into the Delta office as well: one from the Delta Unit day room or living room and the other from the Echo Unit day room. This is important to note because it is possible for Delta unit inmates to signal Echo unit inmates via these two windows since the two windows into the Delta office are across from one another. During the Rookie's tenure, the Delta Unit office had its desk set up so that both windows fed into the office from the back of the unit officer's desk.

So basically, if the Delta Unit officer was at his desk facing forward, whoever was in Echo Unit, whether it be inmate or DOC staff, could survey the Delta Unit officer at his desk undetected unless the officer turned around to catch them looking in at him.

On one evening just after the Rookie CO completed his unit lock-in, (in bed / lights out at approximately 10:30pm), the control room operator radioed him to say that he should step out into his unit hallway and clear it, as inmates were not in their cells. His exact words were, "You need to clear your hallway. They're not in their rooms." This seemed a little strange to the Rookie because he could usually tell by the sound coming from the hallway if his unit was compliant or not. While in the Delta Unit office, CO's would usually have the door open, allowing them to hear what was going on in the hallway. He had also just checked the hallway moments prior.

The Rookie knew, however, that the camera was there to help him and initially felt reassured knowing that the control room operator was watching his back. After all, he was a rookie and had much to learn; knowing that the officer in the control room was helping him run his unit made him feel like his fellow staff were there helping him. On this occasion, as on others, he was mistaken.

Since the Delta Unit office door was right there on the hallway, securing it and making the requested check only took about forty-five seconds. In order to comply with the control room operator's request, it took the Rookie the amount of time to close the office door, walk the length of the hallway and check that nobody was in the bathroom, then walk back down the hallway to the unit office. He made sure that all the cell lights were off; there was no noise coming from any of the cells and he noted nothing suspicious.

Upon returning to the Delta Unit office, the CO noticed that the Delta Unit Logbook was missing. They teach every CO to guard this diligently as it is a legal document where the unit officers record every headcount, each security check, any issues in the unit, the behaviors of inmates, basically anything for that unit. For the first several minutes, the Rookie thought that maybe one of the inmates had figured out how to get into the Delta Unit office during those few seconds to steal the log. But then he realized that the control room operator had the camera on his back. Or did he?

The Rookie CO called the control room operator to see if he saw any inmate enter or attempt to enter the Delta office while he was walking down the hallway in the opposite direction. This would have been the only time that anyone could have even tried to get by the Delta office door, which was locked. To the Rookie's dismay, the control room operator said he didn't have his camera on his unit when he made the requested hallway check. He had, however, the

Delta Unit Floor Plan
Conceptual Diagram

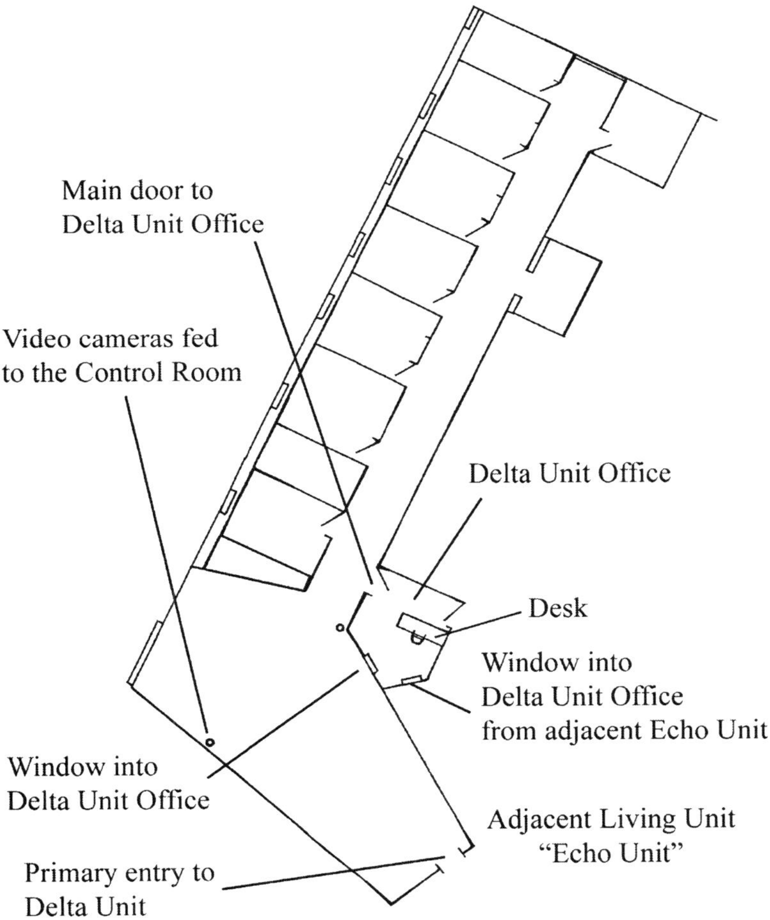

camera running on his unit hallway long enough for him to request the check in the first place.

The Rookie CO continued to check his unit but remembers very well that he had left the logbook right where he had been trained to do so. It's either in the top drawer of the unit office desk or on the right-hand side of the desk. It is usually accompanied by a clipboard with the unit headcount sheet attached. In this case the Delta Unit officer kept the clip board with him, as that's what he was trained to do.

For the next forty minutes the Delta Unit officer searched his unit and office for the log book. Then just before the end of his shift he received a phone call from his supervisor S1 Mayberry, saying that he had his logbook.

The Rookie CO believes that another officer working in conjunction with the control room officer used the request to clear the Delta Unit hallway to lure him out of his office so that another officer (believed to be CO Blatick because he returned it later) could enter the Delta Unit office via the adjacent Echo Unit doorway to make off with the Delta Unit logbook undetected.

It should be made clear that nothing is ever taken out of a unit without letting the unit officer know about it, particularly something as crucial as the unit logbook.

The Rookie mentioned to his S1 supervisor that it seemed a little ironic that his log book was not only removed from his office without him being informed but that it happened at precisely after the time he was called out by the control room operator. As the Rookie later found out, the culprit had entered via the door to his office from the adjacent Echo Unit as to avoid the Rookie's detection. The S1 vehemently denied any wrongdoing on behalf of his subordinates.

At that, the Rookie didn't want to create a scene nor cast any suspicions upon his fellow staff members, so he immediately dropped it. There was no doubt in his mind, though, about what had happened. No one removes a unit logbook unless the S1 requests to see it. They certainly don't take it without asking and informing the unit officer. When his S1 phoned to say he had his logbook, the Rookie could hear the laughter in the background and a chuckle in the S1's voice to boot. When CO Blatick returned the logbook, the Rookie could see the little smile on his face, as to say, "Don't worry, here it is."

After that, the Rookie CO wrote the normal checks in the logbook under the remark "After the logbook exercise" because he felt as though maybe staff were trying to teach him a lesson so that he'd keep the logbook with him at all times, which isn't really the way he was trained.

He felt he needed to log the incident because he was trained to log everything. His instructors would say; "If it's not in the log book it didn't happen." Well, it did happen, and it happened exactly as described. It's in the log.

The next day while finishing his shift, he was verbally reprimanded for writing the "After the log book exercise I briefed the incoming CO" remark in his log book. He was accused of being "sarcastic" by a FTO or field training officer Rick Knopp. Officer Knopp went on to say that "That he should have never have mentioned that he was hoping to pursue his Master's degree in criminal justice" and that "It was all over the facility that the Rookie CO was student of criminal justice." The Rookie never wrote anything about this in his logbook, but did mention it to another officer earlier in the evening. Officer Knopp made it sound as if this former CO was in the wrong to have said anything about this. Even though the new CO couldn't understand why, he could easily see that officer Rick Knopp had real distain for him.

Officer Knopp continued to say that "As it stands now, the only other CO remaining from your class is turning out to be a much better CO than you."

It should be noted that the Rookie officer mentioned his intentions on pursuing his Master's degree about *three hours prior to the log book incident* in the Delta Unit office. This happened while he was on the phone with one of his fellow officers and only after he was specifically questioned about "What he wanted to do with his undergraduate degree in Criminal Justice." He mentioned it only one time. It wasn't as if he were bragging or boasting in any way. The Rookie officer said "I'm hoping to pursue my Master's in the same field."

He remembered also that it was S1 Mayberry and CO Knopp who initially interviewed him at the facility in December of 2006. They were the only two individuals to have reviewed the Rookie's full portfolio and resume, both of which articulated all of his education, his prior research, and lists all of his skills and accomplishments, including numerous letters of reference. Some interviewers call this a "brag book" as it includes more than your resume. The reader should have faith that this individual was not bragging; he just wanted the job. Even though it was not a career goal of his to become a correctional officer, he figured with his BS in Criminal Justice he could become a Vermont State employee and perhaps return to his original field of teaching for the state some day. He thought that if he could return to his original field of studies, he could move forward with his career in which ever way possible.

The Rookie CO also sent the commissioner of corrections an email message about his desire to incorporate his experiences at the facility into his master's thesis. The commissioner responded by quoting a corporate executive of his years back: "Let's concentrate on the job at hand." The Rookie took this as a kind of "mind your business" type of statement. It was clear that the commissioner of corrections did not really appreciate the Rookie's motivations to excel in the Vermont D.O.C., and the Rookie was snubbed. After that, the Rookie just left it alone and figured that if he would make it through his first year, then he might try contacting the commissioner again.

The ALPHA Unit Incident

At The Chittenden Regional Correctional Facility, Alpha Unit is the segregation unit where inmates are either being punished and removed from their previous living unit, placed in administrative segregation, protective custody, or isolated for other security reasons. During the two weeks posterior to his graduation at the VCA, the CO "shadowed" other officers in their units. This period was similar to the two weeks prior to the VCA where he "shadowed" out of uniform to give him an idea of what to expect, except now the Rookie CO was graduated from the Academy, was in uniform and further along in the training process. Each day during these two weeks he would be assigned a different officer to shadow. During one of these shadow shifts, he was assigned to Alpha Unit during 3rd shift, from 11:30pm until 7:30am. At this time it is very quiet in Alpha Unit as is the rest of the facility. During 3rd shift there is minimal traffic, and most of the CO's time (in addition to regular duties) is spent completing tasks that the unit officers don't have time to finish during the day, such as administrative duties and record keeping. In Alpha Unit there are only 8 separate cells housing a total of 16 inmates when the unit is at its maximum capacity. This was the one and only shift (eight hours) the Rookie was ever trained in Alpha Unit.

After the two shadow weeks posterior to his graduation at the VCA, he was assigned to the Delta Unit 2nd shift as previously described. This was his full-time assignment everyday unless working overtime and covering for an absent officer. During the second half of March, the facility had a "shift change," meaning everybody is assigned a new unit and shift. Officers may bid on the most desirable times after thirty months of service.

The Rookie CO noticed that the only other officer still remaining from his class at the Academy received a very easy and desirable assignment as "Float." It is considered one of the more desirable positions as the Float has more flexibility and isn't locked in a unit with the inmates. The Float Officer doesn't receive a unit differential of 70 cents per hour more because he's not assigned to a living unit and his responsibilities entail relieving the unit officers for their breaks; thus he "floats" through out the facility. All CO's assigned to a living unit, receive an additional 70 cents per hour for working in a unit. However since a Float Officer is not in a living unit they don't get the additional pay. One correctional officer mentioned that "Unit work is the only thing that matters." He said this because it's in being a Unit Officer that one actually gets to know the inmates and is subject to their behaviors with greater consistency.

The Rookie CO had no preference to what unit he was assigned to and was eager to take on whatever his superiors assigned, in this case "LRO" or "Leave Relief Officer." The LRO receives a different assignment everyday. The LRO must cover for whoever is absent or calls in sick. The Rookie was assigned LRO during 1st shift. He thought this would be good because he'd be able to see the facility's operation in full swing and could get to know the front office staff, as this is only shift they work during the facility operation.

After about five weeks of working different units as LRO per the facility's needs on different days, on April 16th 2007 he was assigned to Alpha Unit. This would be his first time in the unit since his shadow training during 3rd shift two-and-a-half months prior. As always, he accepted his assignment without complaint or hesitation.

April 16th 2007 was a Monday which is one of the busiest days of the week at Chittenden Regional Correctional Facility. There is much more traffic in and out of the units because inmates are being processed in and out at higher volumes than on most other days of the week; The inmates either have court dates or legal obligations requiring their transportation in and out of the facility. On April 16th 2007, there were 22 inmates in Alpha Unit, well over the 16 inmate capacity.

If there were ever a time that was the complete antithesis of his one-time, quiet shadow 3rd shift two-and-a-half months prior, this would be it.

Even though the Rookie CO was busy, he managed to do quite well according to one other officer. It was very hectic. Not hectic because inmates were misbehaving but because it appeared as if many other officers in the facility were constantly telephoning the Rookie about things he'd never been telephoned about.

The Rookie got one call from the booking officer who apparently was calling to see "How he was making out in there." At first the Rookie thought that was nice but then noticed she was laughing to herself while she spoke to him. Without coming across as paranoid, the Rookie felt as if he were being watched and that he had even been sent a few extra inmates to burden his load.

He thought this again when he noticed that his 29-year veteran S1 Jake Milford was looking in on him every couple of minutes through the Plexiglas unit door, kind of chuckling to himself. He'd then bring another inmate in. This happened at least three times while the Rookie was running Alpha Unit that day.

Not long after that, CO Hicks would bang the Alpha Unit door very loudly with his fist as to startle the unit officer.

Alpha Unit Floor Plan
Conceptual Diagram

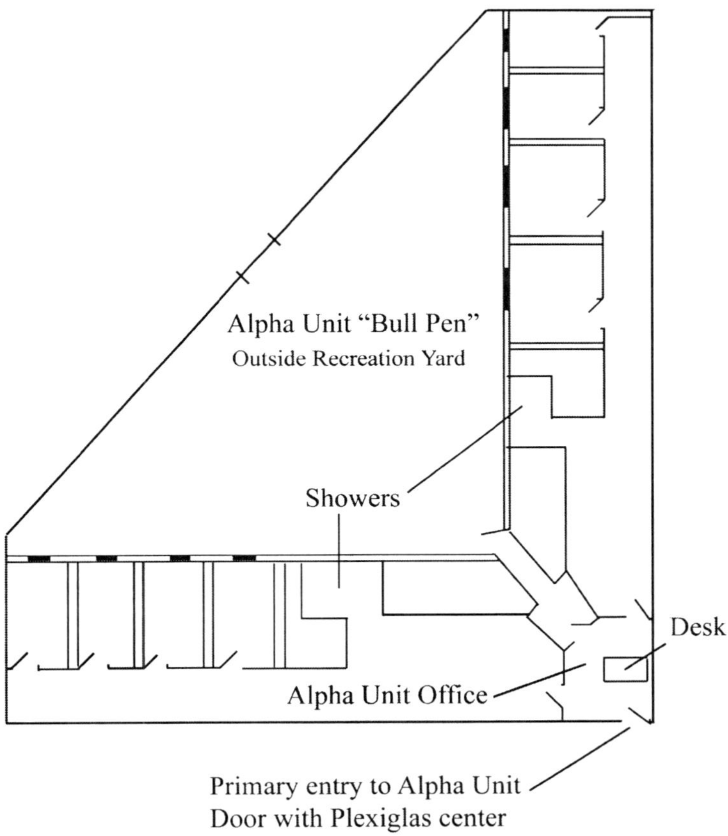

This activity is "An old favorite" at CRCF, as it totally scares the hell out of the Alpha Unit officer because his back is immediately adjacent to the inside of the Alpha Unit door. It should be noted that this activity not only disrupts the Alpha Unit officer from his work, but within the correctional environment maybe traumatic for the Alpha Unit officer as it is very loud.

If inmates are caught engaged in this activity (pounding the Plexiglas unit door), they are punishable by way of a major DR or disciplinary report. The Rookie learned that apparently there's no disciplinary action taken for fellow staff engaged in this activity or at least there was not when he mentioned this to his then-supervisor S1 Jake Milford. In fact, much to the Rookie's surprise, the S1 laughed.

Despite this harassing activity from his fellow staff the Rookie CO managed to perform his duties quite well. He didn't let it bother him and it even motivated him to work harder.

Correctional officers must complete frequent visual checks on inmates for various reasons. Since inmates are in the custody of the State, it is the State's responsibility to guard them against self harm, harm from other inmates, to provide security, and the like. These checks are usually done in intervals of 10, 15 or 30 minute. They are staggered to prevent the inmates from knowing exactly when the next check will occur. In Alpha Unit on April 16th, there were several inmates "on 15's" and the rest of the 22 inmates were on standard 30-minute checks.

As always, the Rookie CO completed these checks as instructed. That day, however, during that period of the shift, so many inmates had been escorted in and out with such rapidity that it would not have been possible for even the most experienced CO to have learned all of their names. But that is what you are supposed to do because if you are checking on an inmate then you should know who they are.

At the end of his shift, he was notified by his then-supervisor S1 Jake Milford that the Rookie had marked his initials (as being checked) twice for two thirty-minute checks on an inmate who had been removed from the unit one hour prior. That's how busy he was. In Alpha Unit each time an inmate is removed from the unit the Unit Officer must call over the radio to have his cell-door opened by the control room. Then he must do the same for the main Alpha Unit door. After that the Alpha Unit officer must start a new check sheet for the new inmate and make sure he doesn't mark any other absent or removed inmates as being checked as present.

With Alpha Unit being set up as two separate hallways with four cells per hallway (both with cameras feeding into the control room) with a 22 inmate load, is only possible that the Alpha Unit Officer make his checks and them note them when done. Apparently the Rookie marked two of his 30-minute checks on an inmate that had been removed with the others coming and going.

For that, S1 Jake Milford said, "I'm removing you from the unit." He didn't say he would like to train the Rookie further for that type of high traffic or that he did a good job considering the amount of inmates that day. He was making it as though the Rookie CO failed at his duties or was incompetent. It appeared to the Rookie that this was his goal the entire time. To the best of the Rookie's knowledge, Alpha Unit never reached a 22 inmate load after that. It was if to deliberately overload a unit the Rookie had never worked in, and been trained in only once, two-and-a-half months prior during 3rd shift. When his S1 Jake Milford removed him from the unit, he just thought, "Well, at least I won't have to go through that again."

The Rookie CO openly admits that he logged two of his initials for two thirty-minute checks on an inmate that had been removed prior. He does not deny this. He acknowledges his mistake, for that's all it was, a mistake.

It was easy for the Rookie to see that it was his staff deliberately trying to over load his unit and make his job more difficult than it needed to be. By that point, it was obvious to him that his support team was amusing themselves by intentionally trying to make him fail. He suspects that this was their goal the entire time.

The ICE and TRASH Incident

Article twenty-four of the *Vermont State Employees' Association Handbook for the Corrections Bargaining Unit* identifies and explains the requirements and parameters of on going training classes officially identified as "Corrections Competency Training."

The Vermont Department of Corrections offers these training or competency classes which the CO's often refer to as "stipend" training because they are paid a "stipend" of $35.00 per hour to take the class. If a CO hasn't completed a state-required portion of his or her training after a specified period of time, the CO is notified that he or she must complete the "stipend" class within a certain time. The reader should note that it looks good on COs' files when they take as much stipend training that they can. The Rookie signed up for all the "stipend training" being offered. In fact, he was the only CO at his facility to complete the training for H.I.P.P.A. (Health Information Privacy Protection Act) which wasn't even required of CO's. After the Alpha Unit incident the Rookie correctional officer figured he might have a few extra challenges come his way, so he was sure to follow every rule and procedure as he was trained to do so.

He observed that when he inquired about several of the training classes, his fellow officers discouraged him from attending under the pretext that "you already had that at the Academy, and you won't need to take that training for another whole year". He thought to himself, "The Academy was 3-4 months ago and why not brush up on it?"

He took them all. Whatever the subject was, if he wasn't scheduled to work during that time, he'd take the class. Because he wasn't through his initial six-month probationary period, he wasn't eligible to earn the full stipend; he could, however, receive overtime for it. Since his mother, father and sisters are all high school teachers and he was a former teacher himself he thought "Why not? Maybe I could teach that someday." The Rookie's father was a teacher for over thirty-five years as was his mother. His sister is currently a special education teacher and his first career was teaching overseas so with this background the Rookie easily identified with the educational and training aspect of the classes.

THEN, about two weeks after the ALPHA Unit incident, he reported to the Control Room to get his assignment for that day, as LRO officers usually do. He was amazed to hear that he was finally being allowed to "Float." As previously described, that meant he'd do all the tasks required for that position and not be locked in a unit unless relieving a unit officer.

He was enthusiastic because he was trained twice for that position and remembers the satisfaction he got from relieving Unit officers and responding to the requests of the Control Room for assistance. Float Officers would also be called to booking for the intakes of new arrivals and whatever else maybe needed, including backup, should a 10-33, (an emergency) be called over the radio.

One of the first tasks a Float does is "Ice and Trash." This is when the Float Officer calls the units over the radio to have each send an inmate with their unit's portable ice cooler and any bags of trash to the shipping dock area which is in the receiving hallway near the ice machine. The inmates leave their trash inside one of the two doors with the other trash bags to be removed and then individually load their coolers with ice. Inmates use this ice for beverages consumed within their living units.

After the inmate from each unit leaves with his ice, the Float officer follows the standard security procedures such as locking the first door behind him before unlocking the outside door, and then disposes the pile of trash bags left by the inmates. The Rookie CO was trained twice as Float and remembers that the two individuals training him had the inmates leave their trash in two different spots at the dock. Even though the result was the same, they had two different procedures.

This was not a big deal because the only real difference was where he would have the inmates drop their trash bags. The first time he was trained in that position, the inmates put their bags of trash around the corner on the trash dolly. The second time he was trained, the training officer had them drop their bags of trash just in front of the door on the floor outside of the room where the trash dolly was. Either way, he would end up securing both those doors and removing the bags of trash himself. There was not a whole lot of space between the two spots, yet one was inside the first security door on the dolly and the other was just inside the first door.

Let us be clear that he'd performed the task just fine which ever way he completed it. After all, he was trained both ways. For the record, he completed the task perfectly.

Then after all the inmates left with their ice and the Rookie CO was about to begin the trash-removal portion of his task, he noticed CO Steve Campbell walking by.

He knew CO Campbell fairly well (or at least he thought) because CO Campbell trained him to run Delta Unit, as he was a former Delta Unit officer. CO Campbell was also a "FTO" or Field Training Officer. An FTO is supposed to be your "GO TO GUY" for rookie correctional officers. These people have achieved the qualifications to train individuals in their field.

Since the Rookie correctional officer knew that CO Campbell was a veteran of the facility, he figured he would ask him which way was the best way to do the trash. After all, he did not want to mess up his first shot as a Float officer. He also knew that CO Campbell was ***his*** FTO, and these were the people of whom you were to ask questions.

This is exactly what happened. The Rookie politely and professionally asked his FTO Steve Campbell which way he thought was the better way to perform the trash removal portion of his duties. CO Campbell politely and professionally responded, telling him that he thought the dolly way was the best. The Rookie CO thanked him, and CO Campbell said, "No problem at all," and went on to say, "If you have any other questions, please, don't hesitate because that's what I'm here for." This took all of 20 seconds. The Rookie felt reassured knowing that his original facility trainer was there for him. He then completed his task knowing that he was doing it exactly as it should have been done.

About fifteen minutes after completing the ice and trash, the Rookie CO was called via radio to the control room. When he arrived, his S1 Jake Milford was there in front of the control room operator Bob Wipple, who was chuckling to himself. Jake Milford informed the Rookie CO that he was removing him from the position of Float Officer "For not knowing how to complete an ice and trash run."

The Rookie CO didn't really know how to respond. Initially he thought that his S1 was joking with him. He tried asking his S1 what he specifically did wrong, but his S1 just responded by saying, "Look, the Float position is really important, and we can't have you in that position if you don't know how to do it." His S1 then reassigned the Rookie CO back into a living unit.

After his shift, he went to speak to S1 Jake Milford about removing him from the Float position. He was very respectful with his S1. He explained that the question he asked CO Campbell was only a "make sure question" and that it didn't prevent him from completing his task. He explained to his S1 that he only asked the question about the trash because he wanted to be the best CO possible. He wanted to do the best job he could. He asked his S1 if perhaps there was something else he did during his duties, something that he wasn't aware of, that motivated his S1 to remove him from the Float position, and his S1 said, "No."

The Rookie CO spoke to several of his fellow staff about this, and their reactions were varied. Some of them just rolled their eyes at the Rookie, and some of them seemed amused by his being singled out.

By this time, the Rookie CO began speaking with his family and friends about his experiences at CRCF. He knew he was still under his initial six-month probation, and the last thing he wanted to do was create problems. One of his friends mentioned that he should start documenting all of his experiences where he thought he was being harassed by his fellow staff. At first, this was difficult for him because it entailed recapturing events where he was being harassed. If he were to maintain a positive attitude and keep his performance up to snuff, he'd have to let certain things go, as he did with the inmates. That is to say he didn't want to let it bring him down. He did a good job at this, in fact, because he continued to work more hours each week, and the few colleagues that were making his job more difficult, he just ignored.

Multiple incidents with Officer Hicks

One of the Correctional Officers at the Chittenden Regional Correctional Facility was Officer Hicks. CO Hicks, as the Rookie CO later learned, was one of S1 Jake Milford's "pet CO's." When the Rookie reported several incidents to his S1, Jake Milford, he was unaware that a particular relationship existed between CO Hicks and S1 Milford, a relationship of "favoritism." As the Rookie CO discerned later S1 Jake Milford's two "pet CO's" were CO Hobbs and CO Hicks. According to several other CO's at CRCF this favoritism existed long enough for it to become common knowledge amongst the DOC staff employed there.

S1 Jake Milford was the primary S1 during first shift at his time of employment, so if the Rookie was being harassed, such as the banging on the Alpha Unit door as to startle the Alpha Unit officer, the Rookie had no choice but to report it to his S1 Jake Milford.

S1 Jake Milford probably had more years of experience at CRCF than any other Correctional Officer in the facility. His seniority has been described by other S1's as "God-like status." Ironically S1 Jake Milford is the "Facility Pastor" at CRCF. He wears the pin of the Mother Mary on his uniform. In the end, the Rookie would have a hard time believing in that this individual could contribute to such dealings amongst his fellow staff, especially rookie CO's who have successfully graduated from the Academy. This is a perfect example of the irony (or maybe ambiguity is a better word) to describe the S1 Milford's status at CRCF.

Numerous times the Rookie was harassed by CO Hicks and sometimes would mention it to his S1 and other times would just let it go because it became obvious to him that the much younger CO Hicks was just amusing himself. On one occasion CO Hicks arrogantly confided in the Rookie that his job was secure in the Vermont D.O.C. and he "could never get fired from his job." As the Rookie CO learned, once a CO passed the initial six-month probationary period, he can not get fired. One could however "get put under investigation" where they're not allowed to show up for work but still get paid. The Rookie CO thought, "Maybe that's what he's trying to do, get put on paid leave." One of these times was when the Rookie CO was assigned to work with CO Hicks.

While assigned as OSR or "Outside Recreation Officer," CO Hicks was noticeably unhappy that he had to work with the Rookie. While preparing for his assignment that day, it was CO Hicks's responsibility as S2 to train the Rookie. During Outside Recreation, the S2 is the officer positioned outside the perimeter or double wire fence. It was here that CO Hicks told the Rookie that he should take the handcuffs off of his utility belt because "the OSR officer isn't allowed to have cuffs on." He waited until the last minute before going out to tell the Rookie to remove his cuffs from his utility belt. He did this right in front of the then Control-Room-Officer Rohnson who heard him say this. Since the Rookie CO knew that CO Hicks was at times playing tricks on him, he waited to see if CO Rohnson's reaction was peculiar in any way as to make sure CO Hicks was telling him the truth. He did this because for him to remove the cuffs, he'd have to disassemble his entire utility belt to remove the cuffs and case. He couldn't just remove the cuffs from the case and leave the case on his belt because hand cuffs were issued by the facility and returned in their case, always. That was procedure.

This took an additional 3-5 minutes to do correctly. After he had the cuffs removed and utility belt back on he proceeded to return them to the Control Room Officer (who keeps them). It was just then, while smiling, that CO Rohnson (while laughing with CO Hicks) told him that he did in fact need his cuffs and that it was only the S2 that didn't need his cuffs. So the Rookie CO had to disassemble his utility belt **all over again** to have his cuffs back on his belt. All of this made him late for his OSR assignment.

Of course his S1 Jake Milford showed right up at that moment to say that he was moving too slowly and that he had to "Move a little faster." The Rookie CO learned from another CO that same day that CO Hicks was complaining that he had to work the OSR assignment with the Rookie and that he "wasn't going to train him on anything". This explained to the Rookie why CO Hicks didn't say a word to him that day, and when the Rookie asked questions of the OSR officer, about the procedures he didn't really get any straight answers. CO Hicks kind of just avoided him. The Rookie CO just thought that he might have been having a bad day, but then learned from other CO's that he was "Bad mouthing the Rookie CO". The Rookie inquired as to what specifically CO Hicks was saying about him but the other CO's declined to be specific. Judging from CO Hicks's actions though, the Rookie didn't doubt it.

On another occasion while working the H-1 unit towards the end of his shift, CO Hicks showed up under the pretext that he was his relief officer. The Rookie CO looked at CO Hicks to make sure this wasn't just another one of his antics. But CO Hicks looked serious about it and seemed sincere so the Rookie gave him the benefit of the doubt. After all it was just about the right time for his relief to show up despite it being about ten minutes early. While the Rookie began to remove his radio to give it to his relief officer, CO Hicks even started to ask the questions a relief officer would ask such as "anyone on 15's?" This is a standard question when one officer relieves another, where the incoming officer is to be informed of the inmates who are on 15 minute checks. These are the same types of checks that were described in the Alpha Unit Incident. The Rookie answered all of his questions and gave him his brief of the unit. Then CO Hicks told him he could go ahead and leave.

The Rookie said he still had ten minutes until shift's end and asked him if he was sure if that was okay. CO Hicks replied, "Yeah it's fine Go ahead." So just before the Rookie left he started to note this in the Unit Log Book. He began to write "Being relieved by CO Hicks early, and he said it was okay for me to go." But then as CO Hicks saw that the Rookie was writing this in the log book he immediately grabbed the log book from him and said "What are you doing? Don't put that in there. I was just kidding."

He then grabbed the Rookie's pen from him and crossed out the log entry the Rookie just made. The Rookie CO honestly believed that CO Hicks was in fact his relief officer. He didn't have any reason to believe otherwise because CO Hicks appeared to be acting sincerely. After CO Hicks left laughing, the real relief officer showed up to relieve the Rookie. CO Hicks did this procedure twice on two separate occasions while the Rookie was working at (CRCF).

The Rookie CO thought to himself that maybe CO Hicks was the facility "prankster." To the best of the Rookie CO's knowledge, however none of his other victims' performance were affected by his actions as were his. Hicks's other targets certainly weren't in their "initial six-month probationary period."

Incident at 0330 hrs

The Rookie CO knew he wasn't in any way perfect nor did he ever pretend to be. He made a concerted effort to fly below the radar. The fact that he was willing to become a Correctional Officer (a career many would never consider) particularly at this stage in his life when he was just looking to settle down and mature a steady career, was in itself testament to his work ethic and his desire to prove himself as an exemplary state employee. One of the mistakes he made was that on two separate occasions, he was late to his shift. He always called in to announce that he was on his way. Both times he made sure that his administration used whatever amounts of "sick time" allotted to him to cover for the minutes he wasn't there. This wasn't more than three quarters of an hour total. He was never once a "no show." Officer Knopp would often be there when the Rookie showed up to work, deliberately looking at his watch so the Rookie would see him checking the time. Officer Knopp would also talk down to the Rookie in what appeared to be a deliberate attempt to "belittle" the Rookie. He'd say things like "Wow, you just barely made it, any later and you'd have been a no show." It would have taken much more than Officer Knopp to make the Rookie a "no show." The Rookie was never a "no show" for anything in his entire life. He just wasn't raised that way. CO Rick Knopp seemed so ever anxious to accuse him of being late, deficient and inadequate so many times. It was easy to see that instead of working with the Rookie to train him, Officer Knopp would go out of his way to try and make him fail.

One of the ways the Rookie ended up being on time, was to call in during the second half of second shift to see if anyone called in sick for third shift. Eight out of ten times there was someone "Banging out" as they used to say. "Banging out" is slang for calling in sick. This would allow him to cover the "back half" of third shift for the covering S1. This would mean he'd show up for 0330 and work four hours of overtime just prior to the beginning of his regular eight-hour first shift.

This would allow him to work a 12-hour shift, giving him much-needed overtime to supplement his paycheck. It would force him in at 0320 so that he'd come into the facility at a much earlier, calmer, and quieter time than his usual 0720 time. It would demonstrate that he really wanted to work. In most cases, he would call the facility asking if the slot was open instead of waiting to see if he'd get called. He did this quite often as it was conducive to his lifestyle. He'd just go to bed a little earlier and then get up at 0230. He was never late again for one of his shifts. . .

Well, not quite. He was late one other time and here's how it happened.

It became routine for him to try to work a 12-hour shift by coming in at 0330. On one particular morning he showed up to "cover the back half of third shift." He showed up at about 0320. Since the facility was quiet during these hours it gave him ample time to pick up his utility belt, punch in, and get to the unit he was covering.

At 0320 in the morning, CRCF is locked down, meaning one had to buzz the control room officer with the outside intercom to have him call staff to let him in at the front door.

The control room officer could not just open the door electronically, or if he could, he never did. He always sent a Float officer up to the front door to let staff in. The control room officer could see who was up front via one of several cameras often trained on the front door location.

So while showing up for one of his "four hours early" shifts, the Rookie CO buzzed the front door. The control room officer, Mack Bouin said he'd have staff "be right there" as he always did. This, however, is what happened.

It was taking much longer than normal for staff to let him in. The Rookie had been standing up front for an additional four to five minutes before ringing the buzzer again. The control room officer again said, "He's on his way." Then after another several minutes he noticed that CO II Merrell Nealson who had been the "Acting S1" all week during 3rd shift was making his way to the front door. He noticed that the CO II was laughing to himself on his way up to let him in. This is what happened next.

When CO II Merrell Nealson pushed the front door open, he said "What are you doing here? You're not on The schedule." The Rookie CO said that he was now late and had to hurry... While standing in the doorway the CO II again said "No, you're not. Trust me You are not on the schedule."

At this the Rookie CO looked at CO II Nealson whom he assumed was still the supervisor for that week. Acting S1 means that he's filling in for an S1 that's either absent, on vacation and or he's practicing for a future promotion to that S1 position. CO II Nealson looked sincere and yet appeared amused because now the Rookie CO had gotten up in the middle of the night for nothing. Again the Rookie CO said he was pretty sure he was filling in for someone who'd called in sick. They write one's name on the schedule as soon as one commits to filling in for someone. So there was no chance of CO II Nealson being honestly mistaken, as the Rookie's name had to be on the schedule even though he was filling in for someone else.

Then once CO II Nealson was just starting to really convince the Rookie that maybe he did make a mistake somehow, the Rookie said hesitantly "Okay, but I better not get in trouble." At that the CO II still standing in the doorway said, "Go home and get yourself some sleep and come back in a couple of hours."

Then just as the Rookie CO was turning around to head back towards his car, the control room officer who'd apparently been watching this on the camera, quickly announced over the intercom, "Get in here. You're on the schedule." At that the Rookie looked at CO II Nealson knowing that he had been lied to. He sarcastically said, "Thanks, Nealson." Officer Nealson got a big chuckle out of this.

Thinking that the S1 for that night was CO II Nealson (as he had been for the whole week), he'd just hurry to his unit as it was Officer Nealson who had made him late and would not penalize him. Because of this, he punched in at approximately 0334 and didn't get to his unit, which was Bravo Unit until, 0337.

Upon his arrival into Bravo Unit, however, and much to his distress, the Rookie CO learned that CO II Nealson wasn't the acting S1 for that night; it was S1 Jake Milford at the officer's podium, waiting for him.

S1 Jake Milford said, "You still haven't corrected your tardiness, have you?" The Rookie CO didn't want to be defensive because his S1 was right: he was late. When the Rookie tried to explain what had happened at the front door, Jake Milford became somewhat bellicose and started saying that he had to write him up for being late. The S1 went on to say, "When staff keep coming to me and say that other certain staff are late, then it's my responsibility to do something about it." The Rookie was amazed to see that this 30-year veteran was actually part of setting him up. S1 Jake Milford then "wrote him up."

The Rookie was having a hard time believing that an almost thirty-year veteran of the facility, a man who held rank in the Catholic diocese and was the Facility Pastor would engage in such an activity. This wasn't the first, second, nor third or fourth time that his S1, Jake Milford appeared to be singling him out by deliberately impeding his job performance. The Rookie CO did not believe that his S1 had been motivated to part take in these activities on his own, but rather to not question those veterans of his facility who were informing him about the Rookie. In the Rookie's mind, they obviously took advantage of his trust in them to harass the new-comer.

Later during the end of his first shift at 1530, the Rookie CO went to speak to Milford to make sure the S1 knew why he was several minutes late that morning. He told his S1 what happened at the front door and explained that it was CO II Nealson who contributed to him being late. Jake Milford said exactly this: "It doesn't matter. You're still responsible for showing up to your unit on time." That was the end of that.

The Rookie told this to his Vermont State Employee Association Representative, Abigail Mitchell, who said that he should have mentioned this to his "union steward at the facility." The problem with that was, the Rookie's union steward was CO II Merrell Nealson, the same guy who set the Rookie up at the front door. She basically said, "There's very little you can do," and she openly made comments about how this type of thing has been going on for a long time. She didn't seem surprised at all. She said to the Rookie CO, "Oh yeah, I can believe it. Trust me."

The Rookie asked her if this is something that they're allowed to just get away with, and she said; "Until your initial six-month probation is over, there's very little you can do."

Turning Positives into Negatives

For historical purposes and in an effort to objectively preserve his moral integrity, the Rookie decided to document the various tactics that veteran staff used to manipulate his performance. Even though these events have been recorded for legal purposes, not all of the tactics encountered nor incidences of harassment are represented here.

One tactic veteran correctional staff used at the Chittenden Regional Correctional Facility is yet another example of how security staff assimilated to the behavior of their inmates. The Rookie CO observed on numerous occasions when his performance was exactly to the VCA standards, he was inexplicably reprimanded. In many cases he noticed that not only did certain veteran staff plain out ignore his exemplary actions but often would try to make it out as if he actually did something wrong, when in fact he was performing exactly as he was trained to do so at the Academy.

Incarcerated populations have been known to behave in such a manner to their fellow inmates. If they are threatened by someone or need to discredit them, they start by circulating false information about them as to immediately defame their character. This is done in an effort to mislead others from the truth and often includes turning a positive into a negative. Unfortunately for the integrity of DOC staff, they've assimilated this tactic into their treatment of newly graduated correctional officers.

Corroborating this phenomenon on page thirty-one of the *2005 Report on factors contributing to the high attrition rate of correctional officers* in Vermont, summarizes that "Bad performance was recognized but good performance was not." The report continues on the same page; "Contributing to poor performance were lack of teamwork, back biting and favoritism. The phrase 'good old boy system' came up in several narrative responses." Within the Job Performance Feedback section of the same report, page twenty-five recommends; "Recognition of good performance and stronger messages that line staff are valued and respected. Don't react just when someone does something wrong."

Several of the following chapters will describe a few such incidents where his fellow staff employed this tactic on him. In these incidents the Rookie believed that it was in fact his S1 who did this to play down his performance as inadequate or substandard, when in fact it was exemplary.

The Contraband Stop

In late spring while being relieved to use the bathroom, the Rookie was asked by the control room officer to screen an emergency package in. This meant that the Rookie CO was to go to the front of the facility and go through the items brought in for an inmate by either a family member or friend of the inmate.

Even though the VCA had a segment on searching for contraband, most of it was centered on searching the cells of inmates. The VCA did cover searching and patting down inmates. Other than the paperwork and enforcing which items and how many were allowed into the facility, there was never any in-depth facility training on the procedures involved for screening packages. The Rookie CO knew, however, what to do because he did get some help from a fellow CO who showed him the procedure about a month prior when the Rookie had been asked to screen a package.

On this occasion, a father was bringing clothes in for his son. The Rookie CO informed him that he could only bring in a maximum of two of each item of clothes for his son, e.g., two pair of sox, two pair of shorts, and pants and shorts with five pockets weren't allowed.

Screening the clothes in emergency packages is a meticulous affair. Inmates have been known to regularly have friends and family members literally sew tobacco, narcotics, and even weapons into the seams of their clothes in order to smuggle them into the facility. The screening officer will use all his senses and more than due diligence to make sure that the articles of clothing being brought in to the recipient inmate are completely free from any contraband.

In this particular case, the Rookie CO found a very small folding pocket knife (whether deliberate or not) in one of the back pockets of some cargo shorts. He immediately looked at the father, who was probably in his late 60's. If the contraband were to have been narcotics or drugs, the Rookie would have been much more suspicious of the father.

After the Rookie CO pointed out the small knife and held it up, the father became ashamed and embarrassed. He knew that he could get in trouble for having that in the clothes, and he also knew that the Rookie wasn't going to let him bring it into the facility. The shorts were also prohibited since they had five pockets.

The Rookie immediately interviewed the father who, to the CO's mind, probably wasn't aware of the pocket knife being there. He politely, yet sternly, told the father that he'd have to take the unallowable items back with him and that if he were caught again with anything similar, he may be considered as attempting to bring contraband into a correctional facility, an action with serious consequences.

After interviewing the father, it was the Rookie honest opinion that the father wasn't aware of the pocket knife. In fact, the pocket knife looked as though it had been through the wash because the plastic casing was smeared with pocket lint. The small knife had also had looked like it had been "banged up" or abraded from going through the dryer. The Rookie felt assured knowing that he stopped if from entering the facility. The father was old and frail, and the shorts that had the knife in them were equipped with too many pockets, anyway. It was most likely a mistake.

While this encounter was winding down, another officer was walking by and heard the Rookie interviewing the father and noticed that he had stopped some contraband from entering the facility. This passing officer obviously told the S1 because only five minutes later, while the Rookie was actually on his way to tell his S1 about his contraband stop, the S1 Milford approached him as if something were wrong.

The Rookie said to his S1, "I was just coming to see you. What's wrong?" S1 Milford said to the Rookie "Why didn't you tell me about this?" The Rookie responded, "I just barely finished and was on my way to tell you now." S1 Jake Milford practically exploded and said, "I can't believe you didn't tell me about this. Now I have to call home office and explain that you didn't notify me." The S1 went on to say, "This is really serious, why would you just let something like that go?"

The Rookie was hoping that the S1 would have done like he's done with all the other CO's who did exactly the same as he did when stopping contraband, and at least acknowledge him for doing so. It was clear that S1 Jake Milford was going to turn this into another infraction. It appeared to the Rookie as it would have anybody else: that his S1 was deliberately trying to turn a positive into a negative. Again the Rookie correctional officer did exactly as he was trained at the Academy, yet it counted against him.

The Rookie didn't want to act boastfully nor in a self-congratulatory way; he just did not understand why his S1 was so pejorative towards his contraband stop. He didn't want to challenge his S1 nor stoke his criticism, so he just acknowledged his S1's remarks and dropped it.

The Performance Evaluation

During the month of May, the Rookie was notified by CO II Mitchell that he was instructed by S1 Jake Milford to write up a performance evaluation of the Rookie CO. At first the Rookie thought nothing of it, but then considered how this evaluation might affect his initial six-month probationary period.

The Rookie respected CO II Mitchell because he always appeared to be open and honest. He remembered that CO II Mitchell had taught *Search and Seizure* at the Academy. Officer Mitchell told the Rookie "not to worry at all" and that "performance evaluations were standard for all Rookie CO's." The Rookie CO learned though that the only other CO still remaining from his class, the one that was a "much better CO" than he, didn't have a performance evaluation required of him.

The Rookie tried to not worry about anyone other than himself. He figured as long as he kept working hard and doing everything that was expected of him, he wouldn't have to worry about his evaluation.

Two weeks passed, and the Rookie still hadn't heard back from Officer Mitchell so he decided to ask him about his performance evaluation. Officer Mitchell said that he was almost finished with it, and he needed to have their S1 sign off on it.

It was the next day that Officer Mitchell gave the Rookie his multi-page performance evaluation, just after his lunch break. Officer Mitchell said to the Rookie, "Listen. This isn't a big deal, but when you're done going through this, I'll need you to sign off on it." The Rookie CO thanked him and said "Okay, fine." Once back into his unit, the Rookie waited until he finished his duties at hand to examine the evaluation. He couldn't help but to see the "unsatisfactory rating" on the first page. It was then that he knew his fellow staff were succeeding in adversely affect his performance.

Once he read his evaluation, the Rookie realized that much of what was written wasn't only extremely subjective but in most cases involved the times when he was being harassed. The evaluation didn't state that he had long since corrected the few times he was tardy but rather mentioned it as if it were still a problem. The Rookie knew that he had been late only on three separate occasions, and the last time was when he was deliberately held up at the front door by Officer Merrel Nealson.

The "performance evaluation" erroneously stated the Alpha Unit incident in which the Rookie's unit was deliberately overloaded as having occurred on April 14th 2007 a Saturday, and not the correct day, April 16th 2007 which was the much busier Monday. Weekends at CRCF are completely different from Mondays in that they are much quieter. The evaluation describes the Rookie's error stating that "the number of confinement sheets didn't match the number of inmates in that particular room" which is true. The Rookie was never trained on confinement sheets.

It became obvious to him that the 22 inmate load and high in-and-out traffic in Alpha Unit that day was deliberate. The Rookie CO understood that Milford was deliberately trying to make his mistake seem more serious than it actually was. He remembered how they loaded his unit with inmates far beyond the unit's capacity and how officer Hicks kept disrupting his work by pounding on the Plexiglas unit door.

The Rookie also recalled while relieving the Alpha Unit officer on June 28th that the Alpha Unit officer Mara Monthier missed four 30-minute checks on one inmate and had suffered no repercussion whatsoever. So why would his two initials on two 30-checks on an inmate that had been removed from the unit be worse than officer Monthier missing four 30-minute checks on an inmate who was still in the unit? Further more, the inmate load was much lower than when he ran the unit on April 16th. The Rookie noted that officer Monthier was treated with great favoritism and that she rarely had to work Alpha Unit.

The "performance evaluation" stated that the Rookie officer "will receive further instructions on improving his performance as an officer and how these types of incidents can be avoided." The Rookie never received any further instructions on running Alpha or any other unit.

The "evaluation" did state some positive aspects of the Rookie's performance; he noticed however, that the "*Values*" page was a total misrepresentation of his performance. Under the "Integrity" section of the *Values* page he read that "Staff find him defensive when given advice." This is yet another deliberate misrepresentation of the truth set in print to mislead those who might read the evaluation into thinking something other than the truth. The Rookie wasn't defensive ever, as he recalls, and the fact that they wrote this about him in his file set off an alarm in his mind; he was realizing that his fellow staff and supervisors were not only fabricating untruths about his work ethic but purposefully defaming his character.

Unfortunately for the Rookie CO and the integrity of the State of Vermont this unlawful defamation of character proliferated through the local community in which he lives. The Rookie was amazed to see to what lengths the veteran staff would go to, to humiliate him. Several days after receiving his evaluation he had been asked by several of his fellow staff, "If he found it easy being a CO?" Some of the staff even approached the Rookie just two days after receiving his evaluation to ask him if he thought it was "everything that he expected it to be." During the same week after receiving his evaluation, the Rookie had several of his friends whom he played hockey with approach him while playing and ask, "hey how's life in the Big House?" While the Rookie admits this could be just a coincidence, the timing of all these interactions along with their tone and intonation while asking their questions told him more than he needed to know. One of these hockey friends knew Lance Horner who was also a hockey player and worked at the same facility as the Rookie.

Later the Rookie discovered that a couple of the CO's working at his facility were spouses of individuals who worked at the local college where his then-girlfriend worked as an assistant professor. For a period of about two weeks after receiving his evaluation, the Rookie received numerous inquiries as to his level of job satisfaction and "how he liked being a CO."

The evaluation concluded with a recommendation that the Rookie's probationary period be extended for 90 days. The Rookie decided to meet with the superintendent on his own to discuss how he might improve so that he could pass the initial six-month probationary period and avoid the extra 90 days. CO II Nealson, the union steward said that he shouldn't go alone; that's what he the union steward, was there for. Even though the Rookie was highly suspicious of CO II Nealson because of his 0330 incident, he did not have a choice about whether he saw the superintendent alone or not. If the Rookie were to disobey his union steward and meet with the Superintendent alone, then he'd be disrespecting his superiors by doing the opposite of what his union steward recommended.

Upon the union steward's recommendation, he met with him and the superintendent to discuss this. Both the Superintendent and CO II Nealson pretended this wasn't anything to worry about and that they both had confidence that the Rookie would "do just fine".

After the meeting, his union steward CO II Nealson said that they would just "play a number's game" with the administration in that they would try to get the 90 days to start from the date of the Alpha Unit incident meaning back in April. This would mean in fact that the Rookie would still pass his six-month probationary period on time and get his scheduled pay raise, and sick-time allowance.

As much as the Rookie wanted to believe his union steward and the superintendent, he knew they were now compiling false documentation on his performance, such as the "file" and his "performance evaluation." They were doing it by repeatedly and deliberately setting him up to fail. His only hope was to keep working hard and to document those events where he knew he was being harassed by his fellow staff.

P.M.I.

Not long after the Rookie's performance evaluation, he was contacted by CO II Mitchell again for him to sign off on what is known as a P.M.I. or performance mentor interview. This is a one-or-two page document that highlights the strengths and weaknesses of each Rookie. It also may note suggestions for improvement.

The meeting or interview took place on June 18th 2007 with S1 Jake Milford and CO II Mitchell. The primary point of the interview was that several of the inmates had complained about him to central office.

It should be noted when inmates are being incarcerated or disciplined, they have very little recourse other than to file a grievance or a complaint against the state. Many complaints and grievances are filed daily at the Department of Corrections, as this is the only way inmates can legally protest their situations. By law, the state must provide the opportunity for inmates to file a grievance. Each unit in a correctional facility in Vermont has grievance forms available to the inmates. Often the complaints and grievances filed by inmates are exaggerated or false. It is their only way to get back at the individuals who detain them.

The Rookie CO met a veteran CO II at his facility that was actually fired because a group of inmates falsely accused him of misconduct. It wasn't until two years after the CO II was fired by the Vermont DOC that he was finally exonerated of the false charges the inmates fabricated. The state had to pay the falsely accused CO II for the time he was out of work and rehire him back at a higher pay grade. This sum was more than a year's salary. The Rookie had the opportunity to listen to how the false accusations of a group of inmates resulted in his wrongful termination from employment.

The Rookie's P.M.I. interview stated that there "have been numerous complaints sent to central office from the residents of CRCF." The Rookie knew that there was one inmate who fabricated a grievance about him, an inmate agitated with him for being disciplined. The grievance was a complete fabrication in every sense. It stated that the Rookie CO was "wrestling" with the inmate and called him names. At no time did the Rookie CO ever touch an inmate unless he was "patting him down" at the request of a supervisor. Even when an inmate would request to have something such as ointment applied to his back the Rookie would simply say, "I'm not allowed to touch you." He most certainly never "wrestled" with anyone. This particular inmate has a pending legal suit against the former CO. The inmate's claims were so outlandish that the former CO believes this inmate may have been motivated by DOC staff to pursue legal action against the Rookie.

This way, to the public it looks like the inmate is the perpetrator, when in fact he's just the vehicle for the staff who are behind the action. Even for the lawyers involved it would appear as though something transpired between the former CO and the suing inmate, such as the inmate being mad at the former Rookie CO for having disciplined him or the like. In this case the Rookie did absolutely nothing to this inmate.

So when S1 Jake Milford and CO II Mitchell mentioned that there were complaints against him, he immediately inquired about their nature. At that, both S1 Milford and CO II Mitchell looked away and changed the subject. It was important for the Rookie not only to identify what the complaints were but to perhaps offer some explanation. If there was any truth to the complaints, this would also allow the Rookie to focus on areas for him improve. The Rookie was never allowed to see the complaints nor be informed of their nature. The S1 and COII withheld the complaints from him, and his inquiries about the allegations were never answered.

The P.M.I. stated also that the Rookie should use caution when communicating with the inmates. The Rookie had, however, always used the techniques taught to him at the Academy which included the use of ACT or *Advanced Communication Tactics*. ACT are the prescribed ways in which CO's should respond to inmates in the course of their duties. These prescribed ways of communicating are mostly for when inmates are "acting out" or behaving in an uncooperative manor. When the Rookie asked his S1 and CO II Mitchell what specifically they might have heard about his communicating with inmates, they would not tell him. The Rookie wanted to ensure he would not do it again. Even though the Rookie persisted in asking about the nature of the complaints, the two officers shied away from his requests. It was as if they were protecting someone or keeping the Rookie in the dark. Maybe there were no complaints. Or maybe his S1 and COII were exaggerating the nature of the complaints. But why hide the complaints from those accused?

The Rookie didn't understand why, if the P.M.I. was conducted for improvement purposes, his supervisors couldn't be more specific about his "communication errors." To improve upon his skills, the Rookie would need to know what it is he was doing that needed improvement. Unfortunately, his inquiries to central office about the complaints were never answered. He was not allowed to see the complaints nor did his S1 or COII identify what it was that he was being accused of by the inmates.

The P.M.I. also stated that the Rookie was becoming "suspicious of some of the staff." This was, in fact, true. The Rookie mentioned his suspicions about certain staff to his S1 and COII because of the harassment he was experiencing. It seemed only natural to the Rookie that with all of the events here described one might be a little wary of his fellow staff.

The 10-33 Medical FOXTROT

The contraband incident in itself didn't really raise the "positives into negatives" alarm for the Rookie. Just because the Rookie stopped a pocket knife from coming into the facility and his S1 reacted adversely to his action, didn't make him realize what was going on just yet. It took several other incidences where he knew he took the correct actions and precautions as prescribed by the Academy. The alarms did not go off until several other events took place in which the Rookie responded as he was trained to do so resulting in a positive outcome, yet his superiors ambiguously found fault with him in some way or another. The Rookie was not raised to brag about himself and never outwardly sought praise for anything. He was doing his job and that's what they pay him for. His fellow staff obviously took advantage of this.

Later in the summer of 2007 the Rookie CO was working Foxtrot Unit. Here an inmate by the name of Kip Kruger had been recovering from a tooth extraction by the facility dentist. The inmate had been complaining for days of pain. The Rookie knew perfectly well that inmates are masters at attempting to deceive the medical staff into dispensing pain medication. Many inmates are recovering drug addicts and will stop at nothing to acquire narcotic pain medication.

It was true that inmate Kruger had obvious inflammation on the opposite side of his face from where he said his tooth was extracted. The Rookie took the necessary precautions, such as notifying the health office of his complaints and if anything happened to the inmate at least the Rookie would be covered for following the proper procedures.

Foxtrot Unit was one of only two units at the correctional facility in which the Rookie worked that had the inmates' meals brought into their unit, as opposed to the inmates going to the mess or "chow" hall. As the Rookie was serving his unit their lunch trays and while the inmates were locked in their cells one of Kruger's cell mates started banging on the door. At first the Rookie just thought they wanted him to hurry up as they were two cells down from being served their lunch. But then he heard the inmates call the Rookie's name to come quickly as "Kruger was out cold on the floor".

The Rookie looked in cell number five and sure enough, inmate Kruger was out flat on his back and appeared to be unconscious. After telling the inmates of cell five to get to their bunks and opening the door to the cell, the Rookie CO said, "If you guys are messing with me you'll be sent to seg." One of the other cell mates responded by saying, "He's really out. Trust us. He just hit the deck." As the Rookie CO initiated several verbal commands and nudged the unconscious inmate's foot to see if he'd respond in any way he noticed that the inmate was, in fact, completely unconscious.

At that, he did exactly as he had been trained: the Rookie called over the radio a "10-33 Medical FOXTROT." A 10-33 is an emergency which is only called when absolutely necessary. A 10-33 "medical" informs the medical staff that they should come too.

Just after the Rookie called the 10-33 he remembered that years ago when he had his wisdom teeth extracted he, too, passed out in the dentist's chair upon his follow-up visit. He remembered that the dentist brought him right back to consciousness by tipping the chair back and elevating his feet which allowed the blood to flow to his brain, bringing it much needed oxygen.

So that's what he did. He announced that he was just going to raise the inmate's feet in the air to allow the blood flow to his head. Sure enough, the inmate quickly regained consciousness.

Let's be clear that the Rookie CO understood that he did not save anybody's life: his staff's reaction, however, to walking in on him while he was elevating the inmate's feet was not really what he had expected. It was kind of like, "What the hell are you doing?"

In retrospect, the Rookie realized that he had forgotten to mention in which cell number the incident happened. But he noticed this under his own self scrutiny. Due to his error it took the responding staff extra seconds to locate the emergency.

The S1 that day did say it "looked a little weird with you having his feet in the air." After his shift, the Rookie was in the S1's office briefing his supervisor on the incident while submitting his written report. S1 Barr asked the Rookie what he was doing "with the inmate's feet raised in the air?" The Rookie tried to explain, but it was fruitless. S1 Barr just raised his eyebrows and shook his head in disapproval. The rumor around the facility the next day amongst staff was that the Rookie CO couldn't run Foxtrot Unit because he had to call a 10-33.

The Pat-Down Gloves

In Vermont a Correctional Officer's uniform includes pants with cargo pockets on the outside of each leg. CO's often carry personal water bottles in these pockets as they are spacious enough to do so. The water bottle may protrude from the top of the pocket, but with the cap secured, it is a convenient way for the officer to keep his water with him. The air at CRCF is particularly dry, and dehydration is something that all officers try to avoid.

Another part of a Correctional Officer's uniform is his pat down gloves. Some CO's now use disposable latex or rubber gloves for patting down inmates. Many veteran staff, however use special reusable leather gloves that are specifically made for patting down inmates. The pat down procedure is taught at the VCA during the *Search and Seizure* portion of Academy instruction. A pat down is when members of law enforcement, including correctional staff, use their hands to "pat down" inmates who maybe concealing contraband such as drugs, or weapons. An older synonym for pat down is "frisk" which is used less frequently today.

Oftentimes, a S1 will instruct a CO to Pat Down an inmate or group of inmates in the search of contraband. This procedure is always done with the CO wearing his pat down gloves.

On one occasion, the Rookie CO caught a virus and was becoming ill. The Rookie was rarely ill, the last time over eight years ago; prior he couldn't even remember the last time he caught the flu or had even a cold. He did remember, though, that he was thoroughly trained at the Academy on "air-borne and blood-borne pathogens." He enjoyed that week of training as he learned a great deal and remembered thinking that he'd have to pay particular attention to keeping his hands clean and not touching his face unless with a paper towel. The Rookie CO also learned about the virus Hepatitis "C" and how hearty it was. As did other CO's, he carried hand sanitizer provided by the front office with him at all times.

He knew he had caught a cold of some kind because he felt terrible. Several inmates and staff also mentioned that he did not sound healthy. To illustrate his work ethic in spite of his ailment, he did not call in sick. Even though he had accrued sick time and knew that if he was really ill (which he was) he could "call in" or "bang out" if he wanted to, he went to work anyway.

Fortunately, he fell ill on a Wednesday just two days prior to one of his rare three-day weekends. It was fortunate because he was able to use those three days to recover so as to not miss any work the following week. The only downfall was that he would miss a day of working overtime on his weekend..

While he was thinking back to his week's assignments just prior to becoming ill, he recalled something happened to him that might have precipitated his illness. There's no way he could prove that it did, but he remembers thinking it possible. It stuck out enough for him to document it.

A couple days prior to his illness while in the dining or "chow" hall, a fellow officer jokingly pulled on the water bottle the Rookie was carrying in his cargo pocket. The joking officer did this while standing behind the Rookie officer, perhaps startle him into turning around. He remembered that the prankster really grabbed the nozzle of his water bottle tightly enough to remove the protective sanitary cover which works to keep the mouthpiece clean.

At the time the Rookie didn't really think anything of it, but he then remembered a small detail that he hadn't recognized until well after that shift: The officer was wearing his pat-down gloves when he grabbed the bottle... The officer had used his pat-down gloves to remove the protective mouthpiece cover to his water bottle when he grabbed on to it.

He tried to remember why he had not immediately thrown the bottle away: Just as the joking officer was walking away smiling, as to say "Ha, ha, scared you," the Rookie was called to help pat down inmates leaving the dining hall, distracting him from the incident.

The Rookie can't prove that there was any intent on behalf of this officer to contaminate the mouthpiece of his water bottle; let's be very clear, however, that the dirtiest part of a correctional officer's uniform is most likely his pat-down gloves. It has been said by numerous instructors at the Academy that pat down gloves maybe even dirtier than the soles of their shoes: Pat-down gloves are used by CO's to pat down inmates while searching for contraband or anything that they shouldn't have. Pat-down gloves are used to search inmates who have been working in the kitchen for many hours at a time. Pat down gloves come into frequent contact with places where inmates try to hide contraband, places such as the crotch, underarms, inside of waist bands, and into shoes. Pat-down gloves are used in booking to go through some of the dirtiest clothing one can imagine.

Clearly, the Rookie can't prove any malicious intent, but he does find it interesting that he fell ill just days after the other CO grabbed the mouth piece of his water bottle hard enough to remove its protective cover WHILE wearing the filthiest part of his uniform, his pat-down gloves.

Incidentally the officer with the pat-down gloves was he who wrote up the Rookie's performance evaluation, Officer Mitchell.

The Booking incidents

Constant Observation, or "Constant Obs" as it has become known, is a procedure used by the state when inmates have posed either a serious threat to themselves or others. It is also used in a variety of other circumstances where inmates require extremely close observation. During "Constant Obs," a designated correctional officer will constantly observe the inmate and note his observations every several minutes on a log sheet. No matter what the inmate is doing, the CO conducting the Constant Observation will log his activity. If the inmate is sleeping then that's what the CO logs on the sheet. The CO conducting the constant observation will do nothing other than observe and record the actions of the inmate.

On July 27th 2007, the Rookie CO was again assigned as Float Officer but then reassigned to the Booking Unit where inmate Derik Rouseau was placed in the restraining chair. The Booking Unit is sometimes called "intake" as that's where new inmates arrive. The Booking Officer that day was Officer Mayberry who was now a CO II and no longer S1. Mayberry was the S1 who had the Rookie's Delta Unit log book after it went missing. He was also the other CO who interviewed the Rookie with Officer Knopp. It is unclear whether Officer Mayberry was demoted to a COII or stepped down voluntarily. The Rookie CO was requested to be the constant observation officer for inmate Derik Rouseau who was in the restraining chair, a device used to restrain an inmate who poses a threat to himself or others. It is outfitted with straps for the feet, arms, hands and chest, thus totally securing the inmate in a seated position. The Rookie CO performed this constant observation until other veteran staff deemed it safe for the inmate to be released about 40 minutes later.

Then Booking Officer Mayberry requested that the Rookie CO maintain a "close eye" on another inmate in holding cell HC-1, Max McGowan. This inmate was being "dry celled" because it was believed that he was "packing a slug," in other words, locked in his cell with the water off so he could not flush any contraband he may have concealed in his anus. Dry celling may include other procedures such as restricted diet and no contact with other inmates. Max McGowan was also naked and handcuffed. He was also under the influence of some kind of narcotic, as he was hardly coherent and appeared to be in a stupor. This inmate had obviously acquired an illicit substance; he was barely able to say his own name.

The Rookie kept a close eye on him, as instructed. He also logged all of McGowan's actions, no matter what they were. The Rookie, however, believed that the official "Constant Observation" portion of his assignment ended with the release of inmate Derik Rouseau from the restraining chair. The instructions he received from the Booking Officer were exactly "keep a close eye on him" [McGowan]. The Booking officer did not say "Constant Obs." He said "keep a close eye on him." Shortly after, COII Hook came into the Booking Unit and spoke to the Booking Officer at his desk. COII Hook then gave a close observation log sheet to the Rookie. It should be noted that a "close observation" log sheet is different from a "constant observation" log sheet. The Rookie noticed that COII Hook gave him an observation sheet for 30-minute checks and not the correct "Constant Observation" sheet for five minute checks. When the Rookie inquired if the status of inmate McGowan was, Close or Constant observation, neither officer, Hook nor Mayberry answered him. When The Rookie asked a second time, both of the officers appeared to be too busy to respond. Both Mayberry and Hook were conversing with one of the

Sheriffs who had brought in a new arrival. Finally he just made his five-minute checks on the 30-minute check sheet given to him.

Just prior to lunch the Superintendent stopped in to talk to Max McGowan. The Rookie asked the Superintendent if he thought the inmate could remove his slug while still in cuffs, and he replied, "He most certainly can." So that's when the Rookie knew that if the inmate thought that he was not watching him, that maybe he'd try to extract it, allowing the Rookie to catch him in the act.

The Rookie observed McGowan trying to position himself in an attempt to quickly extract his slug. The Rookie figured it might be the contraband that he had been consuming that put him into his drunken state. So during the course of his shift, by pretending not to notice him, the Rookie was able to get inmate McGowan to pull his slug out. The Rookie actually caught the inmate after several failed attempts to extract the slug. In the end, the slug he was packing turned out to be only matches, still contraband, but clearly not the source of his stupor.

Throughout the course of the day, several other incidents occurred in Booking as well such as an incident with inmate Digger Holmes. In the cell adjacent to inmate Holmes was apprehended by fellow staff as he tried to conceal contraband drugs. During this incident, the Rookie was asked by S1 Troy Caretta to use the video camera to record the incidences as restraint protocol demanded. The Rookie accomplished each task his S1 assigned him, including a written report on the incident.

The Rookie mentions this because after his shift he was openly criticized for stepping away from his close observation post with inmate McGowan. He only stepped away three times in his eight-hour shift, once being relieved to refill the water bottle of the Booking Officer, once for his

30-minute lunch break and then when he responded to his S1's request to tape the Holmes incident. If the Rookie were to have denied his S1's request for assistance with the Holmes incident in the adjacent cell he would have been refusing a direct request from his S1 during an incident which required immediate assistance.

It's interesting to note how skillfully his fellow staff made it appear that the Rookie wasn't doing his job. No one ever said to maintain a "Constant Observation" status on inmate Max McGowan. They said keep "a close eye on him," and removed the word "constant" all together. Then they made as if the Rookie failed at conducting a Constant Observation assignment. When inmate Derik Rouseau was removed from Constant Observation earlier that morning the Booking staff made it clear to the CO that the Constant Observation portion of his Booking assignment was over. The Rookie was called away from his assignment at least two separate times by his superiors. If he was still being assigned to "Constant Obs" by his superiors, they would never have called him away. Or would they?

When the superintendent came back into the Booking Unit after 2:00pm, he wanted to speak with inmate McGowan. McGowan still appeared to be in a deep narcotic stupor. Yet, much to the surprise of the Rookie, the superintendent was actually attempting to converse with him. The superintendent was asking the inmate (who could barely hold himself upright) where "he got the drugs." The Rookie was standing just to the side of the inmate as trained to do while the superintendent interrogated him. The superintendent repeatedly asked the inmate where "he got the drugs." In the course of this interrogation, immediately after posing the question as to the source of the narcotics, the superintendent actually motioned toward the Rookie as if to try and get the intoxicated inmate to implicate the Rookie as the source of his contraband. To the complete dismay of the Rookie, the superintendent appeared to falsely implicate him in an act of criminal activity. Three separate times within the superintendent's interrogation he tried to sway the intoxicated inmate to implicate the Rookie as the source of his narcotics. The superintendent would pressure the inmate for an answer while motioning his head towards the Rookie as if to get McGowan to implicate the Rookie as the supplier of his drugs. This whole scenario seemed surreal. The Rookie was dumbfounded by the audacity of his fellow staff's, particularly his superintendent's attempt to implicate him for some kind of illicit activity. The Rookie only did as he was instructed and trained to do.

In the last two hours of his shift, the Rookie could tell that something was askew with a few of his fellow staff. COII Mayberry was repeatedly condescending to him, as was COII Hook. By this time, the Rookie had become accustomed to his fellow staff members deliberately setting him up, and he knew that he would just have to rise above it.

About four months prior to this, just after the Alpha Unit incident, the Rookie started compiling documentation of the times he thought he was being set up to fail or being harassed by his fellow staff. If the Rookie was sure he had done exactly as he was trained to do, yet the outcome resulted in anything negative such as a reprimand, removal from a post, or a negative performance assessment, he wrote about it. The Rookie also used a digital recorder to record his notes to himself as to assure a timely and detailed account of the event before he forgot it or became distracted by something else.

Modus Operandi

Modus Operandi refers to the way, fashion or method of operating. In a word it refers to "How" a crime or specific act(s) are committed. As opposed to the "Motive(s)," which simply put, refers to why a crime or act is committed. For example; "What motivated veteran correctional staff to harass the Rookie CO?"

The Rookie started examining why certain staff members (mostly veterans with the exception of a few) wanted to make his job more difficult. What were their motives? Did they want to break him or make him quit? Or was he not assertive enough? Should he be more outspoken about the actions of his fellow staff members? Maybe this was all a test or a hazing of sort, and at the end of his original six-month probation, it'd be all over. Maybe he made himself a target by contacting the commissioner about his Master's degree.

Oftentimes within the correctional environment inmates acquire drugs of "unknown origin." That means the contraband could come from outside the institution, such as from those who have the privilege of contact visits or from medical staff. The problem of illicit drugs entering correctional facilities is ongoing. Unfortunately, but perhaps not surprisingly, correctional officers have been known to bring in contraband with impunity. It is the staff, however, that cover it up. The Rookie believed that the superintendent was trying to deliberately implicate him to cover up something else or the real origin of McGowan's contraband which could have been a fellow CO. He still wasn't sure if this was some kind of test or if his days as a correctional officer were numbered.

Inmate populations are easily manipulated by correctional staff. Inmate populations are in large part either developmentally disabled, mentally ill, or suffer from substance abuse. Because of this, veteran staff developed ways to not only abuse them, but abuse their fellow staff via the inmate population.

An example of this would be, on several occasions the Rookie believes that the staff and superintendent encouraged individual inmates to deliberately act up to adversely affect the mood of the unit in which he was working. These incidents involved times when he was running a "smooth unit," a calm unit. Once an inmate would act up, the Rookie would have to call a "10-25" to have staff "meet" him at his unit for assistance. A "10-25" was almost as serious as a "10-33" which is an "emergency." Calling a "10-25" meant the unit officer needed assistance from any available support staff, but that it wasn't urgent enough to call a "10-33". When Control Room Officers heard a "ten-twenty-five" or a "ten-thirty-three" on the radio, they would repeat the call over the radio along with the requesting unit so that supporting staff such as S1s and Floating Officers would know which unit to respond to. For example a "10-33 FOXTROT" would indicate that staff should respond to Foxtrot Unit. Because this activity was broadcast over the radio, the entire facility would be aware of it, thus drawing attention to that unit and the unit officer who called for help.

Sports enthusiasts have been known to say "the best offence is a good defense." In this case, however, the Rookie believed that the veteran correctional staff at CRCF used the theory that "the best defense is a good offense," explaining the staff's tactics of trying to set him up to fail prior to him being able to expose them for their contribution to the 35%-77% high attrition rates of first year correctional officers.

Inmate populations often try to defame or damage the integrity of others who pose any potential threat to them. They try to "beat you to the punch" so to speak. Before any positive influence could be imposed upon or won over by the "potential threatening" individual, inmates often target them as non-credulous or as someone not to be trusted.

In this case it is a college educated individual that represents the "threat" to the correctional staff. This might be why the administrators of the VCA inquired as to how many recruits had their four year degree. They may have anticipated them being targeted.

How would someone's education or credentials make them such an active target? By now the Rookie CO was well aware of him being targeted by his fellow staff. But he still wasn't sure if it was just a hazing or test of sorts for Rookies. A veteran CO confided in him that there was resentment among some of the veteran staff because it took years for them to reach the pay at which newly graduated CO's started at. The veteran CO asked the Rookie what his pay rate was and wanted to know if the Rookie was thinking of making "a career of it?" For the first time the Rookie CO had real testimony from a veteran staff member on what may be potential motives for him being targeted.

If veteran staff could place in question the competence, moral integrity or overall performance of the Rookie then they could process him out justifiably. They had a whole six months to work with to accomplish this. This document in its entirety shows numerous methods of harassment and character defamation employed by veteran DOC staff. Their methods exemplify that veteran correctional staff assimilated to inmate behaviors without question.

Dismissal

August $13^{th,}$ 2007 was a Monday not much different from others at CRCF that summer. The Superintendent had just returned from a two-week absence. Much to the Rookie's surprise, he was allowed to float for the first half of his shift and was even assigned to Alpha Unit again for the "back half," meaning the last four hours of his shift. This meant that he was finally being allowed back into the position he was removed from during the "Ice and Trash Incident" several months prior. He was happy that he would be allowed to prove himself as a competent Float Officer. The Rookie was also hoping that this meant that he had regained the confidence of his S1 Jake Milford. After all, his S1 certainly would not have assigned him to the Float position had he any doubts about the Rookie's competence. Being reassigned back into Alpha Unit for the second or "back" half of the shift made him feel as though this was his opportunity to re-establish himself as a worthy Alpha Unit officer.

A little wary at first, he noticed that the Alpha unit inmate load was more commensurate to its capacity than the last time he had worked it in April when the unit was overloaded. The Rookie also noticed that he was being treated better by some of the staff that week. Several of the individual staff approached him to compliment him on being more self assured and on having more self confidence. He thought that maybe this was it, that he would make it through his probationary period. He also noticed that several caseworkers at the facility were much more personable to him during the two weeks leading up to that day. They seemed more willing to make small talk and spoke freely about their careers as caseworkers and took more time with him than they had previously.

Then just about fifteen minutes prior to the end of his shift in Alpha Unit, he was relieved by Officer Hicks who wore his usual smirk. Officer Hicks was the younger favored CO of S1 Milford with whom the Rookie endured multiple incidents. Skeptical of this officer because of his previous antics faking the Rookie's early relief, he hesitated and made sure the relieving officer wasn't joking again. Then Officer Hicks said that the Rookie was to report to the Chief of Security's office. Figuring that officer Hicks wouldn't kid about that, the Rookie briefed him on the unit and gave him the unit's equipment: the keys, radio and case, etc.

On his way to the office, the Rookie was greeted by several other officers telling him that they had noticed a big improvement in his performance; they were happy to see he'd made it "on the team." Because of their praise the Rookie figured that he'd probably made it through the initial six-month probationary period and that he was to be affirmed as "off the initial probationary period" by the Chief of Security.

Such, however, was not the case: the chief of security handed him his letter of separation from the Vermont Department of Corrections under the pretext of performance issues. The Rookie was fired. Dismayed, the Rookie CO asked the Chief of Security if there was any one thing that he may have done to deserve being let go. He responded by saying, "We can go talk to the superintendent right now." He then escorted the Rookie to the Control Room to relinquish his ID badge and key-card. The Control Room officer was Mara Monthier who was the officer that missed four 30-minute checks in Alpha Unit and enjoyed much favoritism amongst the S1's. She appeared to be aware of the circumstances as she had the key-card cabinet and ID badge box already open, waiting for the Rookie to turn his in.

Officer Monthier avoided eye contact with him but was smirking to herself as to affirm some inner satisfaction she received from watching the discharged Rookie being put under escort at the loss of his job. The Rookie remembered asking himself; if he were in her position (or any position for that matter) would he ever find satisfaction in someone else's job loss. The Rookie didn't get it, but maybe that was because it was he, who was losing his job and not her. Or maybe it was just because he had worked so hard and overcome so much adversity during the past six months that Officer Monthier's smirking at him exemplified her own ignorance of his situation. Or maybe it was because she was seeing the "college boy" getting fired. Again the words the Rookie was looking for to describe her behavior escaped him. But then he remembered; "*Schadenfreude*."

The Chief of Security then escorted the former CO to the front office to see the superintendent. Along the way, numerous other CO's were looking on. It was easy to see that they had been informed of his dismissal and were here to watch the show.

When the Rookie CO asked the superintendent why he thought that his performance justified his dismissal, the superintendent responded by saying "You aren't CO material, and shouldn't be working in security." The superintendent said that the Rookie "played grab ass" with several of the inmates and that he didn't respect the "boundaries" between the correctional staff and inmate population. The Rookie was shocked.

The Rookie asked the superintendent if he had any specific examples of the "boundaries" infringement, if there was a particular incident to which the superintendent was referring. The superintendent replied "yeah examples like Dilaudid." The Rookie immediately looked up in astonishment and repeated; "Dilaudid? It took the Rookie a few seconds to understand what was happening to him and what Dilaudid was. If the Rookie understood the superintendent's remarks correctly, the Rookie was just accused of bringing in, or having something to do with Dilaudid which is (Hydromorphone) a very highly narcotic opiate pain medication that many inmates would go to great lengths to acquire. At that the superintendent just looked back into his computer monitor. So the Rookie then turned to the Chief of Security with bewilderment and said "What? Are you kidding me?" The Chief of Security just gazed out the window, a strained look on his face. The Chief didn't know what to say and neither did the Rookie.

At this, the Rookie was sure that his superintendent would stop at nothing short of slanderous fabrication to have him dismissed. This was the ultimate in Cultural Assimilations representing the transfer of inmate behaviors all the way up to the superintendent level. As previously mentioned, Cultural Assimilations take place when varied parties (including complete opposites such as inmates and correctional staff) associate, intermingle continuously, or live together long enough that one (usually the minority) starts to take on the characteristics the other. In this case, the correctional staff assimilated to the ethical standards of their inmates, a result of prolonged exposure and interaction within the inmate population. The fact that his highest facility-level supervisor was engaging in total character assassination just to have him removed, proved to the former CO that even the facility superintendent would jeopardize his own moral integrity in order to dismiss the Rookie. None of what the superintendent said made sense nor was it truthful.

Truly saddened, the former Rookie maintained a calm profile and attempted to ask the superintendent what he could do to improve. The superintendent responded by saying only; "You shouldn't be so paranoid and that people aren't always out to get you." Mind you, he said this as he was dismissing him from his employment. The former Rookie thought momentarily, "Who wouldn't feel paranoid?" Not only was the superintendent falsely accusing the Rookie CO of being associated with illicit contraband but he was terminating his employment and slandering the Rookie by trying to associate him with a felony. Additionally he was using false pretenses and his years of state employment to do it. The former Rookie just nodded and said "Okay, I'll remember that."

Now the former CO understood how "Eight out of ten COs were implicated with bringing in contraband."

The former CO believes that the superintendent made a reference to Dilaudid because earlier he had tried to implicate the Rookie in inmate McGowan's narcotic stupor in the Booking unit; this was perhaps a way for the superintendent to reinforce that implication. The superintendent was also trying to place the former CO's integrity in question. The superintendent may have also been trying to justify his actions in Booking by associating the Rookie in some way to inmate McGowan's stupor. This demonstrates another example of assimilation to inmate behavior: if you can cast doubt on an individual's credibility or integrity, you can raise questions about the truthfulness of what they say, or in this case about the Rookie's innocence. Inmates do this all the time.

The Walk of Shame

While being dismissed in the Superintendent's Office, the former CO noticed several other staff members started to gather outside on the sidewalk leading from the main entrance to the employee parking lot. They were all congregating, not leaving the premises as they usually did after their shift. He could see that they were all waiting for him to leave to humiliate him. He could see that those who normally rushed to get out of work were now waiting around, joking and having a good time before they could humiliate the fired CO.

He knew they wouldn't overtly humiliate him, but would throw up a façade of concern and try to smooth over the havoc they put him through during the past six months. He knew that this would be their moment of pleasure.

At this the Rookie openly asked the Superintendent and Chief of Security if he could please wait in the conference room until they left. He found it ironic that the superintendent would have him terminated exactly at shift change. There was no doubt in the former CO's mind that the superintendent planned this to "show boat" his authority and make an example of the Rookie. The newly fired CO thought to himself, "If the state of Vermont only knew this went on." Maybe the state does know, maybe this is what they want. Then he thought that maybe this is how they kept the Vermont Correctional Academy (VCA) in business. If the attrition rate of first year correctional officers in Vermont were to decrease from 77% maybe the VCA wouldn't be able to show the state a need for new appropriations for the Academy. The former CO felt that the VCA had done a satisfactory job when he was there, but let's face it, if they had done **that** good of a job the attrition rate of first year CO's wouldn't be near 35%-77%.

To his surprise, the Superintendent said he could wait in the conference room until he felt more comfortable when leaving. But then barely two minutes had passed when the Chief of Security came in to say, "Okay listen, it's been five minutes, and you should go now." Both the superintendent and the Chief could clearly see the individuals congregating out side via the superintendent's large office window. When this happened the former CO knew for certain that it was the superintendent's deliberate intention to have him paraded before his peers to purposely humiliate him. He was amazed to see this type of mentality at the highest level in a correctional facility. It made the former CO realize that the State of Vermont probably changed the title of the position of "Warden" to "Superintendent" to cover up the lack of moral integrity those in this position sometimes have. "Warden" is a much better title for this type of individual as it has earned a stigma from Hollywood that depicts the cold and calculating stereotype. The writer lays no claim to the actual definition of these two words but rather the social stigma attached to them.

Not in a position to argue, the former Rookie followed the Security Chief out through the front office to the locker room where he emptied his locker and removed his belongings. It still being just after shift change, numerous officers all looked on as the former CO was escorted out of the facility. He was walking the "Walk of Shame."

Despite this, the former CO held his head high and knew that no matter how hard the veteran staff tried to defame his work ethic, education, or character, he had nothing of which to be ashamed. He avoided eye contact with the onlookers because it hurt him to know that the false pretenses on which he was fired would give much pleasure to those staff members who stayed to gloat over his dismissal. Many of these onlookers were the same individuals who took part in the numerous incidents of harassment during the previous six months. The former CO could not only see but feel the pleasure they had in watching him be escorted from the facility.

Lance Horner

Lance Horner is longtime employee at CRCF. The former CO knew Lance Horner as they used to play ice hockey together in a men's league. He also knew, however, that Lance Horner never really liked him that much. Even when Lance Horner was trying to be nice, he still showed animosity towards the former CO, even during their hockey days.

It just so happened that when the former CO was dismissed, Lance Horner was in the group waiting outside to humiliate him. The former CO was polite and respectful as usual, despite having to walk to his vehicle past the multitude of staff that lined his path. Lance Horner asked him, "What happened?" The former CO could hear the pleasure in his voice.

The former CO explained that if his best wasn't good enough, then he'd just have to do something else. After another five to ten minutes of small talk with Lance, the former CO asked Lance to do him a favor. Lance replied, "Sure," The former CO asked him if he could wait as long as possible before saying anything to any of their mutual friends about his job loss. He didn't want to have to start answering questions nor be put on the defensive right away. Lance replied, "Don't worry about a thing. I won't say a word."

The former CO said he'd appreciate this as he was embarrassed to have worked so hard and not make the team. Lance said, "Listen, don't worry about it. I won't say anything."

Within fewer than two days, the former CO had each of their mutual friends come and ask him, "How's work?" One of the former CO's acquaintances came up to him while he was eating dinner at an outdoor restaurant, and said "Hey, how's the job going?" Within the 72 hours after he was dismissed, so many people came up to him to ask him how his job was, he felt it was just better for him to say, "Fine. Thanks for asking." He knew that it was Lance who had informed these individuals about the former CO's job, because one of their close mutual friends confided in him that he heard of the dismissal from Lance.

“Whisper down the Lane”

One of the most popular elementary school games has been around for more than a century. In “Whisper down the Lane,” or “Telephone” or “Telephone Operator,” the participants either sit or stand in a line or circle. One of the participants is given the honor of devising a phrase to whisper to their neighbor so that the neighbor may do the same to their neighbor, continuing down the “lane” to the last person. The person who starts with his or her phrase is referred to as the “operator” or “leader.”

The object of the game is to whisper exactly what one has heard from one’s neighbor to another neighbor who will do the same to the next. It is important for them to whisper to make sure the phrase isn’t heard by their peers. Once the phrase has been passed all the way down the line, it is the job of the final person to announce to the group what they think they have heard from their neighbor, the 2nd-to-last participant. Amusement arises when the participants discover the difference between what they’ve said or think they’ve heard and what has actually arrived at the end of the line.

There maybe a moral or hidden message to the game, but whether children retain or grasp this message for later on in life is debatable. The game is still used today by elementary school teachers as a good short break or as a playground animation.

In a small town, bad news is really “good” news, as it is the bad news that generates local interest and gossip. People do like to hear good news, but let's face it, it is more like a “soft story” on the evening telecast. Even the most admirable of our community's citizens, whether knowingly or not, contribute to the proliferation of slanderous hearsay. One might think that such pillars of the community would not engage in such gossip. It is this gossip that has prompted our lawmakers to pass legislation protecting medical information from being circulated publicly. A good example of this legislation would be the new Health Information Privacy Protection Act or HIPPA. The HIPPA act basically states that health care practitioners, including their staff, are responsible for keeping the private and personal information of their patients confidential. The reason for this is because private medical information can be used against someone with devastating effect. Individuals have been known to lose jobs, miss out on promotions, lose friends and family, and even go bankrupt because their private medical information has been shared with the wrong person or people.

As for HIPPA, it only exists on the books. Small-town medical staff, HR employees, and even physicians have been known to compromise the confidentiality of personal information with the most damaging results to the careers and reputations of patients. Assistants change jobs or get fired, individuals get divorced, and as a 1980's pop band once said, "I know that neighborhood, and talk is cheap, when the story is good."

The Rookie remembers very well that he had informed the Superintendent of his aspirations to return to his original profession of teaching and that he was provisionally slated to teach an online class in the criminal justice program of the local college in Burlington. Located within a short walking distance from where the Rookie CO lives, the college would have been a convenient place for him to teach. That summer, the director of the Criminal Justice program finished his term and moved on to another institution. There was a new director of the Criminal Justice program, and the Rookie hadn't known him very well. The Rookie had met the new director only one time prior and found him personable and interested in his experiences. The new director was a former Deputy District Attorney for the State of Vermont. After meeting him for the first time, the former CO remembers thinking to himself that he'd make a good mentor for his graduate studies.

That fall, however, after his termination by the state, he went a second time to speak to the new program director to reiterate his interest in teaching there. He was hoping that since the previous program director was expecting him to teach a class that summer or fall, that maybe the new director shared the same expectations. Since he was newly unemployed, he needed the work. When the former CO went to speak to the program director, the director was just as polite as before, and he took time out of his day without an appointment. The program director, however had asked him some questions that made him aware that he (the new program director) had conversed with someone else about him. This in itself was not really a big deal. Maybe he had heard good things about him. But this is what happened next.

The new program director asked him, "When were you a Burlington Police Officer?" This immediately struck a chord with the former CO because he never was an actual police officer nor did he ever claim to be. It stated clearly on his resume that he completed his undergraduate internship with the police department, but that was all. When the program director asked this question, he was paying careful attention to the former CO's response and, while doing so, made eye contact with him. At no point did the former CO ever claim to be a police officer, but he did respond by saying that he completed his undergraduate internship with the Burlington Police Department years back. The question stuck out in the former CO's mind because he remembered that several inmates found out that he worked at the Burlington Police Department and consequently, called him "Cop," teasing him about having worked there. Of course, many inmates had a history with the local police department; several inmates who were recidivists and had "run ins with the law" during the former CO's employment at the BPD, knew many of the former officers. Once the inmates established this connection, he felt a need to make it clear to them that he was only completing his undergraduate internship, and that it was for Parks and Beach Patrol, not as a uniformed officer. The subject never resurfaced, and there was no need to ever bring it up again.

The former CO felt that something had definitely changed. The opportunity never materialized for him to teach at the local college, not even an on-line course as adjunct. Each time he e-mailed the director, he could tell that even though he would respond, the opportunity had dissipated. The new director stated that he usually gave his adjunct positions to "fellow attorneys" who he knew in the area. The former CO couldn't help but wonder if the defamation of his character at the correctional facility less than a mile away had anything to do with the director's decision.

Not only was the former CO permanently removed from the list of potential adjunct instructors for the local college, but the superintendent's attempt at justifying his actions with the former Rookie CO included using his contacts at the college to further harm and defame his character throughout the community. About six months after the former CO's termination, the Rookie walked over to the local college to visit a long time friend from his hockey playing days who works there. Though his friend wasn't in, he thought he would stop by to see if the director of the criminal justice program was there to reiterate his interest in teaching the on-line course. As luck would have it, the program director wasn't in either. While walking home the former CO noticed a colleague of his ex-girlfriend (a teacher at the college) who happened to notice him. It was as if she had seen his face on a wanted poster! He tried to think nothing of it, but this is exactly what happened;

The next day the former CO walked over to the college again as the spring semester was soon to start and he remembered the program director suggesting that sometimes there are last minute needs in the spring semester for adjunct professors. Since he still needed the work, the former CO figured he had nothing to lose. Upon exiting the college the former CO saw the college's director of security services, who just so happened to be his former supervisor at the Burlington Police department when he completed his undergraduate internship there. As it turned out, the slander originating at the correctional facility (less than a mile a way) was so vigilant against him, that the harm to the former CO not only included being removed from the tentative list of adjunct professors, (obliterating any hopes of employment there) but prompted the security staff at the college to conspire with the former CO's ex-girlfriend to try and take legal action against him! Not only was his ex-girlfriend swayed by the security personnel at the college to try attack him judiciously but motivated her to lie in court (known as perjury.) Fortunately the judge had her "BS" protectors on and threw the case out. This was a sad day for the integrity of the local college as well as it's "security services."

It should be noted for historical purposes that even though the campus of the local college is a "stones throw" from his house, the former CO was probably on the campus no more that five times within the year. These visits involved his hopes of becoming employed there. The former CO has no doubt as to the origin of the original slander, (the superintendent.)

It is amazing to see what lengths individuals will go to, just to cover up their own misconduct. The proliferation of gossip into slander exceeds all boundaries in small-town America and Burlington, Vermont is no exception. This is, in fact a perfect example of modern day character assassination.

The State "Investigation"

Once the CO was separated from the Vermont D.O.C., he sent the Commissioner of Corrections an email stating that he felt he had been harassed and that there was corruption at CRCF.

About ten days later, a representative from the Agency of Human Services sent an email back stating that he was an "investigator" for the State of Vermont. He said he would investigate the allegations of the former CO.

After several phone conversations with the investigator, the former CO agreed to go to the state offices to speak with him in person about his claims of harassment. The former CO knew that such a meeting might be rather fruitless because, after all, the "investigator" was working for the State and assigned by the Commissioner of Corrections.

The former CO also noticed that prior to going to the state offices to have the meeting, the "investigator" tried vigorously to persuade the former CO to bring in all his digital recordings and documentation for examination. The former CO suspected that the "investigator" was now trying to protect the State of Vermont against potentially damaging evidence which the former CO had accrued over his employment. He told the "investigator" that he'd draw up an outline of his experiences specifically for their meeting but that he would not bring his documentation and digital recordings.

Once the former CO finally met with the investigator in person, he found him to be very cordial. The investigator had the former CO sit down with him at a table in his office.

There was a table-top microphone at the table at which they were sitting, and he asked the investigator if their meeting was being recorded, and he replied, "No, not at all." There was something odd about the investigator's response. The former CO thought to himself that all his experiences involving investigations, particularly where someone is coming in to either speak to a public investigator or elaborate on allegations no matter what their nature, the conversations are usually taped for further evaluation. The fact his conversation at their one-time, face-to-face interview with the state investigator was not recorded or taped just seemed "off" to him.

Immediately, the investigator asked the former CO, "Are you filing any kind of law suite against the State?" The former CO replied "Not as of yet, but I am writing about it." The former CO found it interesting that this was the first question the investigator asked him.

As the investigator spoke and asked questions, the former CO could see that the investigator was definitely defending the State. He tried to make it sound as if the former CO was being "too sensitive" or exaggerating. Towards the end of their two-and-a-half hour meeting, the investigator mentioned several hypothetical scenarios as a potential explanation of why things happened the way they did at the correctional facility.

The investigator remarked to the former CO, "I don't know. Maybe" This happened, or it was because of something else. The former CO initially thought that this was just the investigator thinking out loud to himself as if to give some explanation of things he had no control over. But then the investigator said, "I don't know. Maybe you're not the person you say you are." He went on to say, "Maybe you're not the way you look on the outside and maybe you're a closet hippy." The former CO replied "A closet hippy?" He didn't really know what the investigator meant by "hippy." In the former CO's mind a "hippy" is someone that brought back that 1960's era individual who was; anti-establishment, anti-authoritarian, either ultra liberal or progressive, used illicit drugs and protested the Vietnam War. This was hardly the lifestyle of the former CO.

The former CO thought that what the investigator meant by "closet hippy" was that he had this other hidden side to himself that was some kind of explanation for all his misfortune. That was hardly the case. Maybe the investigator was trying to justify the superintendent's actions by suggesting that the former CO was someone other than he actually was.

The former CO had been raised to be truly civic minded by his parents with the intent of serving his community and country. The former CO would have been an officer in the military had he not been medically disqualified from the armed services. In the former CO's mind, no "hippy," "closet" or otherwise, tries to join the armed services. The former CO spent four years of his life studying Criminal Justice to receive his undergraduate degree. As his first profession he then went on to teach second-year law students the U.S. Constitution. At the same time, he completed his post graduate dissertations at the International Organization of Criminal Police, Interpol World Headquarters. The former CO said to himself: "Hippies don't do those types of things do they?" There was nothing the former CO could have thought of nor said to give credence to the investigator's remarks of him being a "hippy."

The former CO then realized, however, that this remark was commensurate to what the superintendent was trying to do in the booking incident with inmate McGowan. He remembered that the superintendent was actually trying to implicate the Rookie in criminal activity involving contraband or drugs. For the investigator to explain the extensive and relentless harassment of the former CO's supervisors by again placing the moral integrity of the Rookie in question demonstrates the State's desire to defend their belligerent behavior by suggesting that he is someone other than he actually is.

Even if he were a "hippy," which he most certainly isn't, would that justify or condone the actions of the staff that were there to train and support him? Unlike many other veteran CO's, the former CO didn't have any tattoos, piercings, motor-vehicle violations or any other characteristics associated with what he thought the investigator meant by being a "hippy".

The former CO also remembered Lance Horner confiding in him years ago that his wife was a daily user of marijuana. Lance said that he was afraid that someday he might end up on the "wrong side of the bars" because of his wife. So the former CO told the investigator about it. He didn't have any further moral obligations to Lance, especially since Lance deliberately lied to him about keeping his dismissal to himself. For all he knew, Lance Horner slandered him in the facility, and it seemed increasingly likely that he, in fact, had.

The former CO mentioned to the investigator that he had considered implementing a course proposal to the VCA on how to deal with fellow staff. The VCA didn't have any curriculum on dealing with fellow staff, and most of the State required 200 hours involved dealing with inmates, First Aid, health issues, security, and safety. He did speak to the president of the VCA about this, and the president openly said that he'd consider anything that the former CO sent him in the way of a proposal.

When the former CO mentioned this to the investigator, he immediately replied, "It won't happen," and looked away while shaking his head. It seemed as though this struck a chord with the investigator because he disregarded the idea without asking anything about the proposal; he seemed adamant that it would never happen. It was as though the investigator was trying to stop the former CO from actually trying to help the State of Vermont protect its own employees. But then he thought, "If they don't have any more cases like this, the investigator might not have anything left to investigate." Then the former CO understood why the investigator may have said this. If the Rookie were to submit his course proposal to the VCA which would have consisted of no more than a two-hour discourse on dealing with harassment and fellow CO's, the amount of investigations (producing job security for the investigator) might go down, as would the CO attrition rate. This would generate less need for the investigator, and therefore it would make sense that he be opposed to it.

In any event, the former CO just let it go. They finished their meeting, the former CO thanked him for listening and the investigator said that he'd be in touch.

It took about a week or so before the former CO realized that the investigator was just filing the motions requested by the Commissioner of Corrections. It dawned on him that part of this investigator's job was to justify what happened to the former CO during the course of his employment. The former CO thought that since he never heard from the investigator again that it was probably just an information gathering session for the investigator. This way, if anything such as a lawsuit or further allegations were to arise in the future, the State of Vermont could at least say, "Look we've investigated this thoroughly." This was their "investigation."

The Human Rights Commission

In the state of Vermont if you have a complaint or feel unlawfully harassed by an employer, you can file a complaint with the Attorney General's Office. Here a special panel will investigate the claim and inform you of the outcome. If, however, you're a "State employee," there would be a conflict of interest since the Attorney General **is** the State.

So individuals who feel they've experienced discrimination in public housing, temporary shelter, or state employment, must go to the "Human Rights" Commission. Like the Attorney General's office, the commission investigates claims of discrimination, harassment, and the like. However, if you don't fall into one of the several categories of legally protected groups delineated by ethnicity, religion, minority status via sexual orientation or gender, you're wasting your time. If you're a sexually straight, white male with no claims to being harassed because of your religion, ethnicity, or any of the other stated criteria, you're simply out of luck. You're just not "human" enough to be protected by the Vermont "Human Rights" Commission.

This is another way that veteran correctional staff were able to manipulate the system to their favor. They knew that the Rookie CO didn't fall into any of these categories. In fact, that might explain why the only other two college-educated CO's at his facility fell into one or more of those categories. One of the CO's was of a minority sexual orientation and the other suffered from a disability that didn't inhibit him from being a CO. Staff probably knew that they couldn't target these employees because they'd end up playing their minority status card. This would expose the bigotry of the staff, and they wouldn't want that.

About one month after the former CO's separation from the Department of Corrections, he notified the Vermont "Human Rights" Commission. He spoke with one of the counselors about his employment with the Department of Corrections. The counselor was polite and attentive. They spoke for about twenty-five minutes, and the counselor asked him if he fell into any one of the protected categories outlined by the Commission. They both concluded that he did not. The counselor finished their conversation by saying "It seems like a difference of education to me."

The former CO tried to explain to the counselor that he was repeatedly harassed by his fellow staff and tried numerous times to get help but was unsuccessful. He explained to her many of the incidences and outcomes resulting from his harassment, to no avail. It became increasingly apparent to the former CO that even the Human Rights commission wasn't interested in his plight nor motivated to do anything to help him.

The paperwork that was sent to him from the commission pertained to legally defined minority members only, none of which he was. She even confirmed this on the phone with him, as previously mentioned.

Months later, after conferring with numerous attorneys, he again contacted the Vermont Human Rights Commission in an effort to identify the criteria of the individuals protected under the Commission. He spoke again with the same counselor he had talked with previously. This time, per his request, she e-mailed him the list of criteria for individuals protected under the Human Rights Commission. Even though the list was more detailed than her initial explanation, it was still apparent that the Commission just wasn't interested in helping him.

The former CO did notice that the counselor was compassionate in her tone towards him, but she had acted similarly the first time they spoke. The counselor also mentioned that the Department of Corrections had an "Oversight Committee" which kept an eye on the Department. She mentioned that one of the members of this committee was well known for curbing the Department's attempts to "brush things under the rug." According to the counselor and the State of Vermont website, this member was a state senator who was available to contact for help on such matters as the.

The former CO tried numerous times to contact this senator to see if there was a way to explain what had happened to him. She has yet to return one of his emails or phone messages.

It is possible that the Human Rights Commission only takes inquires of attorneys seriously, and even though one has been repeatedly harassed, one might need to be represented legally for the Commission to act; the counselor denied this and said that an attorney was not necessary. The former CO could only speculate, as he knew he explained his situation to the Commission and they weren't the least bit interested. They apologized for his experience, but he "was not a member of their legally protected criteria."

Conclusion

The former CO now understood what the Chief of Security meant when he said "eight out of ten" CO's didn't make it past their first year. He now saw how 8 out of 10 officers would be implicated in bringing in contraband. He experienced first hand with a front row seat how veteran correctional staff used a real problem to falsely implicate those who they've targeted. Most "in the know" agree that the illegal smuggling of contraband into correctional facilities is a serious and ongoing problem. It should be noted however that the correctional staff involved in this type of illicit activity aren't usually those under the duress of their initial six month probationary period.

The former CO could have articulated other events in demonstration of employee abuse, harassment and corruption at the facility in which he worked. In an effort to not abuse his first amendment rights to freedom of speech and for security concerns, the author has left unwritten, numerous chapters worthy of public concern.

To this day, the former CO is the live target of a vigorous campaign of state sponsored character assassination. With no real end in sight the former CO continues to endure threats from state sponsored attorneys and local law enforcement in what appears to be a deliberate attempt to intimidate him and his family. Veteran correctional officers and possibly the superintendent himself have even swayed senior staff and the HR department of the local school where the former CO is currently employed for the sole purposes of disguising their own misconduct and consequently crippling his career and ability to subsist within his own community. The results have been devastating. This goes back to the tactic of trying to place the former CO's moral integrity in question prior to him exposing their corruption and misconduct.

In 2007 the Vermont state legislature came forth in its charge that "Spending on corrections facilities and services is increasing at an unsustainable rate. Therefore, the department of corrections shall develop a plan to decrease the cost of incarcerating offenders."

Subsequently, on December 12th, 2007 the Vermont Department of Corrections presented to the General Assembly of the State of Vermont its "*Plan to Reduce Correctional Costs and Achieve Savings for Reinvestment.*" The Executive Summary of this report revealed that between 2000 and 2007 the Vermont Department of Corrections (DOC) budget increased by 74%. The report showed the significant growth of incarceration within the past ten years. This report was extensive in that it covered not only the historical aspects of crime and recidivism in Vermont but also showed the history of programs which worked and didn't work. The reports' three parts included six strategies for reducing costs for reinvestment. The report also found that corrections' spending in Vermont has been growing in excess of 10% per year. The report analyzed each correctional facility within the state and addressed a multitude of possible scenarios for cost reduction. The report revolved primarily around the states' inmate population and the costs of incarceration. It made reference to the possibility of building an entirely new prison in Chittenden County housing both male and female offenders.

In the reports' vast 156 pages, it briefly touches on the cost of training line staff or COs on page 63. But nothing whatsoever is mentioned as to the high cost of attrition and the cost of replacing those correctional officers who leave during their first year. In all of the reports' eloquence and detail, not one single recommendation is made to curtail the high attrition rates of correctional officers in an effort to reduce costs. The report doesn't even address the high turnover rate. It's as if the report is trying to cover up high turnover rates and the high costs that they incur by completely ignoring them. There is not one section, page, paragraph or sentence of the 156 page report that even suggests the state is losing millions of dollars each year by training and replacing the vast number of correctional officers who leave during their first year. This could be perceived in a variety of ways. Either the State of Vermont doesn't think OR refuses to believe that the enormously high attrition rate of its' correctional officers exists, or that the turnover rate contributes to its' high costs. OR, the State of Vermont will not address it, (as it didn't in the report) in an effort to brush it under the rug and ignore it. Maybe the legislature will buy it.

If we were to take those same 369 officers that left within their first year during 2007 and hypothesize that they be reduced by 50%, the reader could do their own math demonstrating an astronomical reduction in cost. Using half that figure at 184 officers we could calculate the total savings of sending each officer to the VCA which is approximately $7,000. each. Multiply that $7,000 by 184 officers and your total is a staggering $1,288,000. in savings. This number should actually be doubled because under normal circumstances the state would be replacing each officer that left. This demonstrates the reduction in cost for the Academy alone and if we were to take into account **all** of the other costs involved, including training both prior and posterior to the officers graduating from the VCA, the savings would well exceed three million dollars.

In any event it is remarkable that a state legislature would command any state department, in this case the Department of Corrections to develop a plan to reduce "unsustainable" costs which resulted in that department submitting a 156 page report addressing everything under the sun, EXCEPT the costs of training new staff as a result of a 35%-77% turnover rate. Not to mention the fact the report submitted completely ignored it. Let's pretend it isn't there.

For the author, the Vermont he grew up in has changed drastically with its entry into the twenty-first century. Gone are the days of Vermont being the quite, quintessential northern New England state harboring honest officials, Champlain sunsets, maple syrup, and crisp autumn air with a hint of wood smoke. It is true, in reality, some of these still exist however, Robert Frost is dead. As the former CO's state employee representative admitted herself, "The good ole boy network is alive and well in Vermont." Backwoods bigotry has found a firm foothold deep in the network of state employees. Power-hungry backstabbing individuals use their years of employment to abuse, harass, and defame educated new comers, in order to intimidate, and remove them.

Regardless of any change the State of Vermont makes to its employment policies, the socio-demographics of its correctional environs give rise to what appears to be insurmountable challenges in protecting its most valuable resource, its employees.

In this domain, state policies not only allow, but promote the industrialization of its correctional officers by trying to cover up and misinform the public about the true nature of the factors contributing to their high attrition rates. In this particular case, veteran correctional staff use nothing short of libel and vehement slander to cover up their own backwoods "hickabilly" bigotry and misconduct. After speaking with legal counsel, the former CO has since learned that in Vermont, "A hostile work environment is **not** illegal." He thought to himself, "If the public only knew where the real hostility came from."

Unfortunately for the former CO the states' defamation of him hasn't ended there. In a continual effort to cover up their own network of corruption and misconduct they have waged an active smear campaign against the former CO. To this day, Vermont State employees use their community contacts to continue to seriously harm the former CO within his own community, specifically targeting his employment. From the local college where the former CO lost his opportunity to further his teaching career to the local high school where he his currently employed the former CO faces a daily onslaught of calumnious attacks on his credibility and character.

For the veteran staff of the Vermont Department of Corrections, years of dishonesty and insecurity add to the State's tarnish. The State has covered up the targeting of educated individuals in their Department of Corrections under the pretext of inmate hostility. Veteran correctional staff even manipulated an inmate to bring legal charges against the former CO. Not only are the inmates' charges a complete fabrication, but this is happening more than a whole year after his employment ended. This demonstrates how powerful and manipulative state employees can be. This also shows how veteran correctional staff, are able to continue their attack on the former CO well over a year after his employment has ended, under the pretext of "inmate hostility." Well over a year since his employment was terminated with the state, he is still sought out and targeted by numerous individuals either working for or influenced by the Vermont Department of Corrections.

Outside of implementing a course proposal to the VCA, and recommendations to the Association of Vermont State Employees, the former CO has no immediate answers to prevent harassment within the ranks of the Vermont D.O.C.. Since his dismissal from the Vermont Department of Corrections, there has been one individual who has called and mentioned suggestions for improvement and he believes that even this turned out to be a “false flag” or a ploy for future defense. They want to be able to say, “Look, we even contacted him for suggestions on how we can improve.” It would be far easier for the Vermont Department of Corrections to cover up or disguise harassment rather than to make the immense changes needed to protect their employees.

From a pragmatic standpoint, the author would recommend some changes to the Vermont Correctional Academy, but this would be a beginning only. There must be some safety valve for rookie CO’s in their initial six-month probationary period to report harassment without jeopardizing their future employment. To date there are none. There must be punitive consequences for individuals involved in harassing their fellow employees. Individuals harassing rookie CO’s (or any state employee) with-in their initial six-month probationary period (or ever) must face serious consequences other than being placed “under investigation” which is code for when you’re paid for not showing up to work: some consequence.

The State of Vermont needs to rethink their Department of Corrections in an effort to defend its employees. It appears that state politics involve not only lying to the public as to the real causes of turnover, but down right character assassination, in attempt to cover up their own misdeeds. The high attrition rates of rookie correctional officers, and their root causes, have been concealed for some obscure reason, and its costing the taxpayer more than they want to know. Maybe that’s it. Maybe they don’t want to know, and therefore don’t. That is why the author decided to record his findings, so that the public would know.

"The problem is how to achieve its responsible use rather than its irresponsible and indulgent use – of how to get men of power to live for the public rather than off the public."

Robert F. Kennedy

Glossary of Terms

Attrition	A reduction in numbers as a result of resignation, dismissal, retirement or death (turnover)
Collusion	A secret agreement or cooperation for an illegal or deceitful purpose (collusive)
Contraband	Goods exported from or imported into a country against its laws. Prohibited.
Corruption	Something against or forbidden by law. Spoiled, tainted
C.O.	Correctional Officer
C.O. I	The first rank of a Correctional Officer
C.O. II	The second rank of a Correctional Officer
Culprit	One accused or guilty of a crime.
Day Room	The main communal living room in a living unit where inmates may gather to watch television, play games or use the microwave or telephone if allowed.
D.O.C.	Department of Corrections
Living Unit	A separation of living quarters into groups by way of either Administrative Segregation "Ad Seg," Types and severity of

offenders. Inmates may also earn the right to be in a "privileged" unit where they may enjoy employment, extra recreational activities, commissary, visits etc.

LRO "Leave Relief Officer," the acronym designation for the officer that will be assigned to fill in or replace another officer who's absent or unable to perform his/her normal duties.

Modus Operandi Latin; A criminal investigation term for "Way of operating," which may or may not prove the accused has a pattern of repeating the same criminal acts using the same method.

Mis en Place French; "Put in place" or "created for."

Prima Facie Latin; "at first look" or "Upon first glance," "on"

Recidivist Someone who has a tendency to relapse into a previous condition *esp.* criminal behavior (recidivism)

Rookie Beginner or Recruit, in this context a Rookie is a first year Correctional Officer

S1 The supervisory rank of a Correctional Officer

S2 The supervisory rank of a Correctional Officer while

	conducting specific tasks such as "outside recreation officer."
Schadenfreude	A malicious satisfaction obtained from the misfortune of others.
Superintendent	One who has the oversight and charge of something with the power of direction.
V.C.A	The Vermont Correctional Academy which is the institution responsible for training Correctional Officers in Vermont

Printed in the United States
208636BV00003B/1-105/P

9 780615 267548